The

Southern Way

The regular volume for the Southern devotee

Kevin Robertson

Issue 35

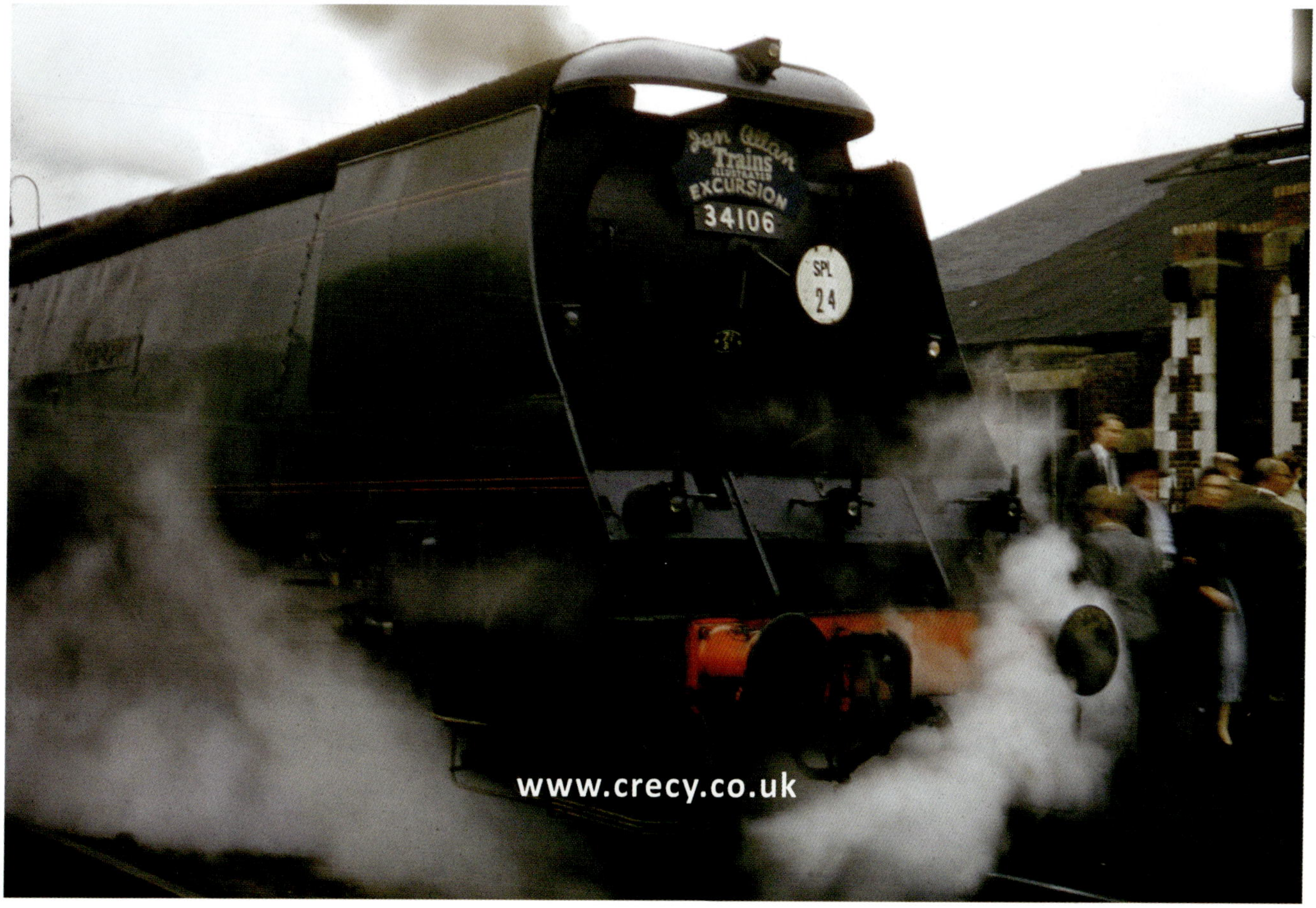

www.crecy.co.uk

© 2016 Kevin Robertson

ISBN 9781909328518

First published in 2016 by Noodle Books
an imprint of Crécy Publishing Ltd

All editorial submissions to:
The Southern Way (Kevin Robertson)
Conway
Warnford Rd
Corhampton
Hants SO32 3ND
Tel: 01489 877880
editorial@thesouthernway.co.uk

All rights reserved. No part of this book may be reproduced or transmitted in any form or by any means electronic or mechanical, including photocopying, recording or by any information storage without permission from the Publisher in writing. All enquiries should be directed to the Publisher.

A CIP record for this book is available from the British Library

Publisher's note: Every effort has been made to identify and correctly attribute photographic credits. Any error that may have occurred is entirely unintentional.
In line with the new design the front cover image has changed from that originally advertised. All other information is unaffected.

Printed in Slovenia by GPS Group

**Noodle Books is an imprint of
Crécy Publishing Limited**
1a Ringway Trading Estate
Shadowmoss Road
Manchester M22 5LH

www.crecy.co.uk

**Issue No 36 of THE SOUTHERN WAY
ISBN 978-1-909328-59-4
available in October 2016 at £14.95**

To receive your copy the moment it is released, order in advance from your usual supplier, or it can be sent post-free (UK) direct from the publisher:

Crécy Publishing Ltd

1a Ringway Trading Estate, Shadowmoss Road, Manchester M22 5LH

Tel 0161 499 0024

www.crecy.co.uk

enquiries@crecy.co.uk

Front Cover:
Almost the end at Midhurst. No more trains to Petersfield and Pulborough, no more race-special and Royal services to Singleton – and no more escaping horses being gently chased out of the tunnel at the east end of the station. Already the signals have gone, the main signal box removed and the former east signal box seen here (latterly the Station Master's office) is likewise redundant. Such was the fate of many country lines in the 1960s although Midhust of course was an early casualty seeing its destinations pruned from the 1930s onwards. Today there is little left to indicate a railway even existed.

Rear Cover:
One of the last active Southern 'Moguls', 'U' No 31639 at Guildford. *Arthur King*

Title page:
The Ian Allan/Trains Illustrated Railtour of 16 September 1956 with Bournemouth-based No 34106 *Lydford* at Salisbury, at the start of the second leg of Paddington–Paddington via Reading, Westbury, Salisbury, West Moors, Hamworthy, Weymouth (and Quay), Easton, Weymouth, Poole, Southampton, Eastleigh, Romsey, Stockbridge, Ludgershall, Grafton and Bedwyn. No 34106 worked from Salisbury to Weymouth – and double-headed with 'T9' No 30707 from Weymouth to Bournemouth – where No 34106 continued alone for the rest of the route to London. It was reported that the nine-vehicle stock for the tour included a number of Pullman vehicles, including a former Devon Belle observation car. The train arrived at Paddington just three minutes late. *NB collection*

Contents

Introduction 5

Charles Anderson 6
    From LBSCR to BR – Part 4
    British Railways, reflections and retirement

Fifty years on 22
    Counting down to July 2017

The Mid-Kent Railway 34
    Part 1

Southern camping coaches 40
    Part 2: 1948–1967

Rebuilt 50
    The letters and comments pages

Terry Cole's rolling stock files 58
    No 34 Some ex-LBSCR push-pull stock

The Salisbury Goods 60

A personal 'bucket list' 66
    Aka – what exactly did happen to No 35004?

Over the Alps '60s style 71

EMU shunting 77

Whistles 79
    Zones of silence

Even more on snowploughs 85

'Bent Bulleids' 87

Colour interlude 89
    Just one station

The Purbeck Clay Express! 94

Introduction

In this issue we (regretfully) come to final instalment of the Charles Anderson story. I suspect I may have mentioned this same point before but, reading through his draft, I am still fascinated by just how much a man in his position had witnessed and been involved in during his career.

I also suspect those in his position (regardless of railway) were the ones who did indeed see the most. Moved from area to area as their careers progressed, they would necessarily come into contact with staff and locations throughout the system. That is, of course, no reflection on the local porter, who might have spent the same length of time at perhaps just one station, nor indeed on the general manager, who observed the railway from behind a desk. But even if such tales as are now being recounted are perhaps few and far between, they stand out and we must be grateful for the information they contain. Now while some of it is no doubt familiar much else is certainly new, which just goes to show how much there is still to learn and (if we are honest) perhaps how little we all do actually know.

Concluding my comments on this subject, I would say that Part 4 is not just a reflection of the final years of Mr Anderson's career but also clearly written from the basis of what were probably diary entries (or perhaps even control logs?), added to which are memories of and comparisons to years past. It is also important to remember that at the time he compiled his notes – probably around the mid-1960s – detailed information such as is now freely available was simply not accessible then and so Mr Anderson's text would no doubt have afforded an insight into aspects of the railway known only to a select few. Rather than attempt to edit and conjoin same, I have instead simply added the very occasional explanation, shown in parentheses, where I consider it is needed. In the same way, his text has been broken into headings and sub-headings. Finally (and as before), there were no illustrations with his draft, which is all the more frustrating because the occasional note 'see illustration' appears in the margin. Did he perhaps take photographs to illustrate his text and if so, have they survived? Instead it has fallen to me to try to find appropriate images. Some may have been seen before, others you may personally know of and think were appropriate but have not been included, usually for reasons of accessibility or cost. Whatever, it has been a privilege to serialise his story, one that I know from many comments already received has been enjoyed similarly by others.

Moving on, July 2017 is an anniversary date that will need no explanation to readers of 'SW'. Notwithstanding what others may or may not be doing, let me say we will be marking the occasion ourselves, starting within this issue and courtesy of a stunning collection of black and white images sent to us by Andrea Durant. The intention is to include a selection of these in each issue leading up to the one for July 2017 (No 39, if I am counting correctly on my fingers) and as the originals were taken at intervals between the summers of 1966 and 1967, it would indeed seem the most appropriate thing to do.

I might add that we also have at least one extra publication due in 2017. There may be two but I am still 'working' on the potential author of the second! I guarantee it or they will be well worth considering; more details a little later.

At this point I had thought this particular missive was complete but then I happened to be travelling by train on Wednesday, 30 March, in the course of which I picked up my free copy of the *Evening Standard*. (Other free newspapers are available!) A piece within the 'Comments' section on page 30 caught my eye: 'Thomas has never been on the right track'. I quote exactly as written: 'Outrage! The new Thomas the Tank Engine film will contain multicultural storylines. Among Thomas's 'very PC new friends' are Ashma from India, Raul from Brazil, and Yong Bao from China. I mean sentimental locomotives are fine, but pink, ethnic ones? Whatever next' … The piece continues, 'The Fat Controller's railway is characterised by a poor safety record and industrial disputes, usually led by a troublesome proletariat (i.e. the trucks) who need to be kept in line'.

So tell me, is it me? If it is, perhaps I don't just need pensioning off but perhaps putting away where my personal thoughts do not risk upsetting or corrupting anyone else. Or the next time I visit a preserved railway or see steam on the main line, will we no longer be allowed to have examples of the 'West Country' class running in case we run the risk of upsetting someone in Kent?

Kevin Robertson

Charles Anderson
From LBSCR to BR
Part 4 British Railways, reflections and retirement

Heading north on the Somerset & Dorset line through Templecombe Lower, BR Class 4 No 75072 heads for Bath on 28 April 1962. *Roger Holmes*

When I was a youngster the doormats at London Bridge bore the initials 'BR' Brighton Railway – and when I finished up they were still initials, although this time the 'BR' stood for British Railways.

The date 1 January 1948, saw the institution of British Railways and regionalisation but the surprise was the re-arrangement of the division or rather district. The Southern District surrendered the West of England Main Line between Worthing Junction (Basingstoke) and Salisbury but took over the Didcot, Newbury and Southampton and Somerset and Dorset lines, so that while the Western Region penetrated the Southern between Dorchester and Weymouth. We in turn penetrated the Western Region north of Cole – thus making it possible to see the Welsh mountains from the Southern District at Burnham-on-Sea. (Note: the boundary changes Mr Anderson refers to were implemented in 1950, not 1948.)

As an illustration of the absurd situations into which the penetrating lines arrangement led us, the following would take some beating. The Queen paid a visit to Dorchester to inspect Duchy of Cornwall property in the vicinity and the Royal Train was scheduled to run to Dorchester West, a Western Region station for operating purposes. The Western Region traffic people said to their publicity people, 'Will you please arrange for flowers to be provided at Dorchester West?' 'Oh, no,' said the WR publicity people, 'we have no locus at Dorchester – you must ask the SR publicity people.' Duly approached, 'Oh no,' said the SR publicity people, 'this department does not arrange the flowers on the Southern – this is done by the Traffic people!' and so I was sent to arrange for flowers to be provided at a Western Region station.

Another queer legacy was the fact that the Southern District worked to three differing codes of block regulations, SR for the greater part of the district, GWR on the DN& S, and LMS on the S&D Line.

Charles Anderson

The S&D Line was a sheer joy. Its history has been excellently described by friends C. R. Charles Clinker and D. S. Barrie but some notes may still be of interest. The layout at Wells was simply incredible. The S&D line from Glastonbury was opened to its terminus, Priory Road, Wells, in 1859 and the East Somerset from Shepton Mallet in 1862 but this terminated in a separate station on the east side of Priory Road itself. The branch from Yatton arrived at Tucker Street, Wells, in 1870 and the two GWR stations were linked in 1873 by the expedient of going right across the throat of the S&D yard. Incidentally, no token was carried by a train between Tucker Street and East Somerset signal box, the signalling between Tucker Street, Wells S&D and East Somerset being done simply by bells. The stations at both Glastonbury and Wells were a long way from the town centres and the branch was closed in 1951.

The signalling between Highbridge and Burnham-on-Sea was a cross between Emmet and the Goons. The GWR main line was crossed on the level by the S&D single line and both up and down S&D platform lines were elaborately trapped to prevent anything going foul of the GWR line from that direction. However, on the Burnham side there was nothing but a stop signal and had a train or engine overrun, it could in a few yards have gone broadside into a GWR train travelling at 60mph – how the GWR let the S&D get away with this I could never understand. There is no doubt that the train staff originally applied from the now derelict box at the WR end of Highbridge (S&D) station to Burnham but once it had gone to Burnham nothing could be exchanged with the GWR or got into or out of the wharf at Highbridge. So the staff were kept at Highbridge 'A' (Church Street) Box and only carried between that box and Burnham-on-Sea, trains being signalled between Highbridge 'C' (S&D), Highbridge Crossing (GWR) and Highbridge 'B' (S&D) by W.R. Spagnoletti instruments and from Highbridge 'B' to 'A' by bell only – three consecutive single line sections without token, the signal box instructions for the latter section bearing the masterly statement that the working was by train staff and ticket except that no staff was carried! Just for good measure, there were no block instruments between Highbridge 'A' and Burnham-on-Sea, as there should have been, merely bells. The difficulty with the train staff seems strangely reminiscent of the FY&N and IWCR at Newport.

I thought I knew something about level crossings with fifteen in 16 miles between Wareham and Dorchester but in 3½ miles between Stalbridge and Templecombe Junction there were seven. On the branch from Evercreech Junction to Highbridge there were actually crossings with no fixed signals, no telephone or any form of warning apparatus – not even a clock. When I had a spare clock I sent it to one of these crossings but got into awful trouble with the Stores Superintendent as I was giving Southern (geographical) Region property to the Western Region!

The Didcot, Newbury and Southampton was an interesting line, too. There was in the District Office at Southampton Central an original map of the scheme, the stations south of Winchester being shown as Twyford, Allbrook, Chilworth, Shirley and Southampton. At the back of Nazareth House, Hill Lane, Southampton, the embankment for the DNS can be seen, while

From 1950, control of the erstwhile Didcot, Newbury & Southampton line south of Newbury passed to the Southern Region. Despite Southern colours appearing on various structures as they became due for repainting, Western Region locomotives (and passenger vehicles) would continue to feature for the remaining life of the line. Here an unidentified 28xx has charge of a northbound oil train from Fawley running through Winchester Chesil.
NB collection

during the Blitz the authorities started to construct a static water tank at the corner of Central Station Road and Blechynden Terrace but had to give it up as they ran into the foundations of the Didcot Railway arches, the existence of which had long since been forgotten. At Whitchurch (Hants) there was until recently a parallel cutting on the north side of the SR station which was to have accommodated a loop from the DNS, presumably with the objective of reaching Southampton via Hurstbourne, Longparish, Stockbridge and Romsey. The LSWR were masters of the art of giving running powers, as witness the District Railway's Wimbledon and Richmond lines, where the District ran thousands of car miles and the SW quietly sat back and drew their not inconsiderable share of the receipts. The same thing happened south of Winchester where the original DNS works were never completed and the LSWR built the costly viaduct across the valley of the River Itchen between Winchester Chesil

Six decades later it is hard to imagine that the road alongside this Standard class 4 is the A34! The engine is in charge of a northbound freight between Litchfield and Burghclere soon after its allocation to Eastleigh. *NB collection*

and Shawford rather than let the GWR have direct access to Southampton. In GWR days that company's station at Winchester was known as Cheesehill, a Victorian corruption of Chesil, shingle or gravel, as in the Chesil Bank.

In 1948, the filthy blue slipper clay found in the cuttings between Lymington Junction and New Milton began to give trouble and the engineer decided to adopt the expedient of blanketing, in effect, digging out the immediate subsoil and substituting 'Meldon dust', the small residual granite from the old LSWR quarry on Dartmoor. For this purpose, we had to give up one line and work all traffic over a short, non-token single line controlled from a temporary signal box. Small adjustments were made in the timings of the trains and the whole scheme worked remarkably well. An interesting side-light: the same trouble occurred on a stretch of Eastern Region main line and the Chief Engineer of that region (an old Southern man) wanted to adopt the same method of working. A deputation from Eastern Region traffic visited Hordle (as the temporary box was called) and were very impressed with what they saw but decided that what might be quite practicable on the Southern with the vast majority of its trains quick-moving, continuous-braked passenger trains, was entirely out of the question on the Eastern Region, where the majority of trains were slow-moving, hand-braked freight trains.

One of the biggest post-war developments in the south was the £37½ million refinery expansion project for the Esso Petroleum Co. at Fawley. The yard at Fawley was remodelled and a nest of sidings constructed by the Esso Company together with a branch line on a sharply rising gradient from sidings to depot proper on which a powerful diesel locomotive operates, always remaining at the lower end of the wagons. Many more millions have subsequently been expended and the refinery and subsidiary schemes continue to expand. For years the line was worked by tender engines but as there was no turntable at Fawley, the engines had to be worked tender-foremost in one direction, not a particularly satisfactory arrangement with the large number of un-gated crossings on the Fawley line. Several types of SR tank engines (including Brighton E6s) were tried with varying success. The real solution lay in the BR Standard tank classes 2 and 3 until the arrival of the diesels.

In June 1949, a through train from Cardiff was running between Broadstone and Poole when fire broke out in the leading coach, presumably caused by an ember from the engine alighting on the gangway hood. The fire spread rapidly and the coach was quickly evacuated and detached in Poole yard where, despite determined efforts to save it, the coach was completely gutted. It was fortunate that the consequences were not more serious.

Some time back, when the Clogher Valley Railway was closed, there was an interesting radio feature on the subject entitled, 'We never lost a train'. Neither have I but I have lost an engine. On the foggy morning of 26 August 1949, the mixed 8.05 train from Glastonbury to Bridgwater, consisting of LMS class 3 0-6-0 tender engine No. 43260, a bogie composite brake, one wagon and goods brake, was running between Ashcott and Shapwick and at a point where a light 60cm track from the Eclipse Peat Works crosses the line on the level, collided with a petrol tractor that had stalled in the gaps between the 60cm and the standard gauge tracks. The line at this point runs

B4 No 30083 assisting in the expansion of the sidings at Fawley refinery. *SC Townroe/R Blencowe collection*

between parallel water courses and the train engine, becoming derailed, plunged into the 20ft wide land drain on the off side, the enginemen fortunately jumping clear. The engine settled down at an angle of 45 degrees to the horizontal with the chimney just above the water and the trailing driving wheels at the foot of the bank with the tender on terra firma but in a vertical position. The vehicles and tender were removed without difficulty but the engine posed a problem. The Motive Power Department had recently recovered an ex-Brighton 'Terrier' in somewhat similar circumstances on the Kent and East Sussex by using two big breakdown cranes (one at each end) but when this was suggested at Ashcott, the Chief Engineer pointed out that the line rested on what was virtually one big sponge and that before he would allow the cranes to operate, special footings would have to be provided at a cost amounting to well over four figures. In the circumstances, it was decided that it would be cheaper to remove as many parts of the engine as practicable and cut up the remainder by oxy-acetylene jet, which was done. As my old chief Hoyle used to observe, 'You never know what is going to happen next on a railway.'

Early in 1950, an up morning express train was in trouble with wheel slip whilst ascending the bank between Christchurch and Hinton Admiral, although the morning was fine and dry. A tank car of gas oil on a previous up freight train had been left with the bottom discharge valve partially open and the escaping oil was liberally splashed over the metals.

Over the trials of the 'Leader' class of engine in 1951 we will draw a decent veil [Pity – ED!] and instead record the advent of the first diesel shunting engines at Eastleigh. Those in the 'Field', 'Tipton' and 'Top End' yards were an immediate success but a more powerful type had to be provided in the East Yard, where the machine has to work against a gradient of 1 in 400.

On Sunday 20 July 1952, an up main line semi-fast train was running on the up local line between Eastleigh and Shawford with a boat train not far behind. The intention was to let the boat train precede as from Shawford, where the four lines converge into two, thus the through line signals were cleared for the boat train and the local line signals kept at danger. Unfortunately the driver of the semi-fast misread the signals with the result that the train ran into the sand-drag overshoot line and the engine – the unlucky ['Lord Nelson'] Class No. 30854 *Howard of Effingham*, plunged down the bank, coming to rest on its side. Fortunately no one was hurt and the tender and leading vehicles were removed without much trouble. The recovery of the engine was not so easy but it was a triumph of ingenuity on the part of Stephen Townroe, the Assistant District Motive Power Superintendent, and Arthur Sheldon, the Assistant to the District Engineer. The metals of the overshoot road were extended on a sharp falling gradient to the level of the engine and the problem was then to right the engine – so it was back to Stonehenge. A pit was dug under the engine on the wheels side and a jack placed under the boiler on the other so that it collapsed into the pit upright. However, before this was done, bull-head rails were wired on to the wheels with the flanges in the web channel. All that was then necessary was to slew the temporary track to meet the bull head and cut the wire. A tractor with a capstan attachment was positioned at the top of the bank and the engine slowly drawn up with a wire rope ten days after the initial mishap.

The only occupations of the running lines (and the local line only) were for drawing off train and tender in the first place and for the ultimate re-railing of the engine. After the Bourne End mishap [30 September 1945], the LM Region had to use all four roads and two or three powerful engines with

Kelbus tackle to right the engine and draw it up, while the expedient of wiring rails to the wheels apparently never occurred to them. The WR was later glad to follow the same procedure after the Didcot accident [on 20 November 1956].

In September 1952 we undertook another combined operation at Southampton Terminus. The 163 lever frame in the Yard Box had reached the end of its useful life and was badly out of line, so the Signal, Traffic and Engineer's Departments went into a huddle and evolved a scheme for putting a new frame into the old box whilst keeping traffic moving, the whole work being completed in eleven working days and nights. (A view of the exterior of this signal box appeared on p56 of *SW31*.) The train service was drastically reduced but all essential services were covered, sometimes with a bus link to and from the Central Station. A small ground frame box with fewer than a dozen levers was installed to cover the essential points and the rest of the movements were controlled by a carefully drilled squad of relief signalmen. As the work progressed, the signal people were able to give us certain facilities and the whole job was completed to time, without the slightest mishap and with a minimum of inconvenience to the travelling public, it being remembered that the Terminus Station handled quite a substantial workmen's traffic to and from the Docks at the time.

In November 1952, six months before the closure of the Gosport branch to passenger traffic on 8 June 1953, Fort Brockhurst had its finest hour, when the Queen alighted there from the Royal Train en route to the Fleet Air Arm at Lee-on-the-Solent. For the return journey, the train left from Fareham. A few days before the royal journey, Waterloo received a telephone message from one of the Queen's ladies-in-waiting saying that the Queen had received a very touching letter from the mother of a crippled girl, who was born on the same day and at the same time as the Queen and would we find a good place for the girl in her wheelchair. The station master at her home station put the girl in her chair in the leading end of a pull-and-push train bound for Fareham where she had a special place inside the barrier and the smile she received from a Very Gracious Lady made up for a lot.

In May 1953, the whole Merchant Navy class was grounded owing to certain defects coming to light and LMS Class 5s and LNER V2s were used in their place until the trouble was overcome. Gloom was cast over our Coronation festivities by the death of Edwin Burrow, who on his retirement from Assistant at the Docks, took up local affairs and died a few days after completing his office as Mayor of Southampton. At the memorial service, my Chief and I were a few minutes early and the Chief, idly flicking over the pages of the hymn book, caught the number 222 and immediately thought of Marylebone Road, the hymn being (believe it or not) *Ten thousand times ten thousand*.

No 30854 *Howard of Effingham* at Shawford just minutes after running through the sand-drag and rolling over in July 1952. Although acknowledged as of limited quality, the rarity factor warrants their inclusion together with this contemporary note from Stephen Townroe, 'One Sunday afternoon in July 1952, a young man sat on Shawford Down watching trains on the main London–Southampton line. Before his eyes a 'Lord Nelson' class left the up track, ploughed down the side of an embankment and turned on its side in clouds of steam. He had a camera and his photographs of a steam locomotive within seconds of crashing were surely unique. What happened after the crash was almost an anti-climax. Mercifully no one was hurt, not even the driver and fireman, who were able to crawl out of the overturned cab. The up through line signal had been cleared for a Southampton–Waterloo boat train, which stopped when its driver saw something had happened. Within minutes the stranded passengers and their luggage were transferred into the boat train and were on their way again'. *SC Townroe collection*

The Coronation Naval Review on Monday, 15 June 1953, was a triumph of organisation. We had worked hand in glove with our Docks colleagues for months previously and everything worked perfectly. Yes, it is true there was an engine failure at Micheldever on one of the last down specials but the train still connected with the scheduled boat and apart from this we had almost a right time working.

Although we operated a small improvised Control from the District Superintendent's Office at Southampton Central on summer Saturdays, our full Control scheme did not come into being until the war years, when it was located in a large concrete structure near the western portal of the Southampton Tunnel. After the first heavy raids on Southampton, an additional but comforting 6ft of concrete was placed on top but however safe or otherwise it might have been under wartime conditions the health of the Control staff began to suffer from the close quarters and artificial light. A fine new Control room was installed by building out from the District offices and this was brought into use in July 1953. Control on the Southern, with its preponderance of fast-moving passenger trains, is very far removed from the Controls on the Northern lines with their slow-moving freight trains, every movement of which can be recorded at the time. On the Southern, as on the Underground, the pace is so keen that the Controller assumes that everything is working to timetable unless advised to the contrary.

Any signal box, station or yard initiating a delay must at once inform Control, who then take appropriate action. On one occasion, the representative of a technical journal used to Northern Controls visited the Control and was a little puzzled at the peaceful atmosphere prevailing. Whilst he was at lunch, a shunting mishap blocked both lines at Cosham, so that he returned to a seething hive of industry – the Sectional Controller turning back trains at Fareham on the west side and arranging bus links between Portsmouth and Fareham, the motive power man tasked with finding engines to replace those coming off their trains at Fareham instead of Portsmouth and the Guards Inspector finding guards seemingly from up his sleeve. Other Controllers were looking ahead, one for example, telling Bristol that the Portsmouth to Cardiff train would be at least 40 minutes late arriving at Westbury, all this while the breakdown gang with 'Bert' and his big crane was being rushed forward from Eastleigh. What a sp1eaded man Bert Wareham was to work with, no shouting or yelling, just a quiet word to the crane driver and a motion of the hand and 50 tons of inert metal is lifted as it by the touch of a giant – and is there anything more undignified and impotent than a derailed locomotive?

The severe weather of January 1954 caught us very badly, particularly at Southampton Terminus where points and turntable froze one evening and played havoc with the return evening traffic, Two days later the engine of the important 7.20am Bournemouth West to Waterloo failed at New Milton and the only engine available was Class N15X No 2331 *Beattie*, with its chimney facing towards Bournemouth but nevertheless her driver worked the train forward from New Milton tender first in a snowstorm until a relief engine (facing the right way) could be provided; a fine piece of work. For four days I spent most of my time in the Control but it was a fortnight before the snow and ice was entirely gone, when the temperature jumped 22° in just one night.

When old and faithful servants retire they are usually bidden to the district office for the chief to thank them for their services and wish them well. One dear old lady at a country level crossing begged to be excused, as she hadn't been out of the village for thirty-five years! Needless to say, 'Mohammed went to the mountain'.

A familiar scene looking north from the down platform at Winchester City with mails being sorted. The signal box (replaced in 1960) is visible behind with, in the distance, the 'Baltic' siding, which is where the fish had been destined. A few (very) red faces all round resulted at the very least. Track-circuiting would have prevented the incident but it is not thought this was provided until the replacement signal box was commissioned in November 1960. *Roger Simmonds collection*

An extraordinary incident occurred as the afternoon through train from Bournemouth to Brighton was approaching St Denys; the enginemen maintained that three conflicting signals were off at the same time. At the inquiry, it was found that a gang of workmen was putting a concrete fence panel into position, when they let it drop on to a run of signal wires. This was followed by another incident at Winchester City, where a loose van was shunted off the rear of a fish train into the siding but failed to clear the main line, where it remained unobserved in the dark by either shunter or signalman until it was struck by the engine of the 2.40am newspaper train from Waterloo, fortunately without derailment or serious consequences. If it had been a fast train instead of the news stopping at Winchester, there might have been a different story to tell.

The cab yard at Bournemouth West was designed for leisurely Victorian days but in the immediate post-war years, the taxi arrangements on busy Saturdays were a nightmare, every vehicle having to go out the same way as it went in and necessitating the services of four or five railway and three or four borough policemen. With the ready co-operation of two local firms, a private roadway from the yard to another public road was brought into use with almost startling results: one railway and one borough policeman being more than adequate but the most surprising feature was that queuing for trains became unnecessary. In order to allow time to get into and out of the cab yard, taxi men had been bringing their passengers to the station much too early but when they could get out so much quicker, they brought their passengers at a more realistic time.

On 23 September 1954, a nasty derailment occurred at Whitchurch Town on the Newbury line in very similar circumstances to the Shawford affair in 1952. A British Railways Class 4 2-6-0 loco No 76017 heading a heavy southbound freight train got out of control approaching Whitchurch and ran right through the loop into the sand-drag and down the bank. An up passenger train was to cross the freight train at Whitchurch and the up home signal was duly against the passenger train but the derailment fouled the signal wires and brought the home signal off as the passenger train approached. The signalman saw what had happened, ran towards the passenger train with a red flag and succeeded in stopping it short of the derailment, richly deserving the reward we were able to get for him.

The engine lay in a most awkward position on the bank and the first thing that was done was to secure it by a steel cable under the metals to a stout tree on the opposite side of the embankment.

November 1954. On her return from the United States, the Queen Mother travelled by royal train from Southampton Docks to Waterloo. I was stationed in the East Signal Box at Eastleigh and as the train passed Northam Junction my Inspector at that box telephoned that a steam heat pipe between the last two vehicles had come adrift, enveloping the train in clouds of steam. I hastily found an examiner on whose opinion I should have to make up my mind if I was to be the first assistant to send the 'Stop and examine train' for a royal special. It so happened that the Inspector on the train had seen what had occurred and it was he who stopped the train in the station at Eastleigh for attention.

On 22 January 1955, there was a nasty little mishap at Bournemouth Central. An engine [N15 No 30783 *Sir Gillemere*] was standing on the up through line at the west end of the station waiting to go to the loco shed, when the signal on the gantry for the down through line was operated. The driver of the light engine took this as applying to him and gave his engine steam, going back on the up through line until it struck the approaching 6.30pm passenger train from Weymouth a glancing blow, derailing the engine [H15 No 30485] and shearing off the offside cylinder as neatly as if by machine. Happily nobody received anything more than a shaking. [see *Southern Way No 13*, pages 61–68]

February 1955 saw the last passenger train on the Meon Valley Line, which was only opened in 1903 principally to keep the GWR out of Portsmouth and Southampton and was an object lesson in the too-permanent way – the station buildings would not have disgraced an important main line and were originally equipped with acetylene lighting, each station with its

Signalman Ken Alexander received his commendation; this took place in the booking office at Whitchurch Town. Standing behind in the railway issue cap is Eastleigh District Inspector Fred Capon, while the identity of the 'brass' on the left is not reported. *NB collection*

No 76017 after it had come to grief at Whitchurch Town in 1954. Debris from several wagons was piled around, although after this had been cleared and the locomotive secured, services were able to resume. *NB collection*

Awaiting recovery, which took place the following weekend. Having initially jumped clear, the fireman then had to return to the engine to retrieve the token for the single line section from Litchfield in order to restore the line. *NB collection*

separate gas house. The yard layouts were most elaborate, while all the structures, tunnels and bridges were wide enough for a double line – and all that lies fallow. In the US, the cheapest possible line would have been thrown down with old coach bodies for station buildings and, for example, a trestle viaduct instead of the costly iron viaduct at West Meon, that is until such time as the line paid its way and was worthy of betterment.

An unattended level crossing on the S&D line near Wincanton appeared to be nothing but an occupation crossing but on making some enquiries at Taunton, the County Surveyor maintained that it was a public highway leading from A to B. We therefore took the office car and duly passed over the crossing but the farther we went, the more the lane deteriorated and, to cut a long story short, we got bogged down in a marshy field, where there was no semblance of a track and had to borrow a shovel from some cottagers, who had doubts as to our sanity. I feel that lane was the crossing's own protection.

A melancholy feature of 1955 was the ill-advised enginemen's strike. On the first day (a Sunday) only four trains ran in the whole district. Conditions improved a little as the days went by but it was over a fortnight before a settlement was reached and we returned to normal.

July 1955. The 9.20am ex-Weymouth was running at speed near Beaulieu Road, when the engine dropped a big end and limped into Lyndhurst Road. We had the most awful difficulty in shunting the disabled engine as we could not get the heavy fallen rod over the rail of the siding connection.

December 1955. As the 2.40pm ex-Eastleigh was running between Lymington Junction and Sway, it was found that the leading brake of the three-coach set (of which the train was composed) was on fire. By all the rules, the train should have been stopped at once but the crew rightly decided to run on the odd half mile to Sway, where the Fire Brigade was summoned and the coach detached and shunted into the down siding. Had the train stopped in the New Forest the Fire Brigade could not have reached it and the whole train would probably have been lost. We never did find the cause of the fire but suspicion centred on something combustible in a mail bag.

And so on into 1956 when, after fifty years, I formally retired on 30 June after the usual month's leave. The most moving feature of my retirement was a crowded gathering at the Marlands Hall, Southampton, when I was presented with a wireless set, a handsome cheque, an umbrella for my wife and an album containing the names of more than 1,000 of the staff, many of whom I had known for thirty, forty or fifty years but most touching of all the Somerset and Dorset staff – whom I had known for barely eight years – almost to a man.

Then and Now

It is, of course, difficult to relate the whole of one's recollections to one chronological sequence, hence this chapter of random recollections. Let us start with the permanent way itself – and so often the too-permanent way. When, for example, the so-called Sarum (Salisbury) and Dorset Line was built, the right and proper thing was done in connecting the city and agricultural centre of Salisbury with the port of Poole via the important market town of Wimborne Minster, but who of those pioneers could have foreseen the emergence and development of the vast conurbation that is Bournemouth?

Now if it had been possible for those metals to have been skewed from a point about a mile north of Fordingbridge to pass through Fordingbridge itself (and not nearly a mile away), then down the Avon valley to Ringwood, there to connect with the Ringwood–Hurn–Christchurch line … life might have been so much easier. Quite rightly the name of the 'Castleman's Snake' [also referred to as the 'Castleman's Corkscrew'] was given to the original Southampton and Dorchester line, which passed through the prosperous market towns of Ringwood and Wimborne Minster but again, who could have guessed the development that took place on the 8 miles of moorland that separated Christchurch and Poole? – or that Dr Beeching and their own respective managements would consider that the Ashendon–Aynho and Castle Cary–Langport cut-offs should (by 1966) have outlived their usefulness? Fortunately closure of both was eventually recognised as a step too far. When Wimbledon was remodelled in the late 1920s, one of the most important features was the provision of the milk unloading platform alongside the volunteer siding – and yet within years it was derelict. When I first went to the London (West) Division, I actually put some finishing touches to the buildings at Southampton Terminus – and that also is now closed. Likewise I saw the Allhallows branch come and go. As a very small boy, I can also just remember the dismal subway at the old East Croydon and the wonderful improvement effected by the present station – but again now I understand that too is to be rebuilt as hopelessly out-of-date. Once again, are our stations too permanent?

How fortunate the Brighton Railway was in the hands of its Chief Engineer, the far-sighted Sir Charles Langbridge Morgan (1855–1940). The scale on which he built took our breath away at the time but passes almost unnoticed today. His ingenious solution to the problem presented by the awkward site for the

Last rites on the Meon Valley line, February 1955. *Viv Orchard*

Charles Anderson

Sykes Lock and Block in use at Tunnel Junction on 28 September 1957. This was a very unusual signal box in design and controlled the junction of the Docks lines to Southampton as well as what had for decades been the main line: Northam curve to Southampton Central. Within was a frame of just fourteen levers positioned to face west. The train seen passing is westbound on Northam curve towards Southampton Central with the lines to the docks just visible coming in from the left. 'Lock and Block' only applied to the Docks lines with three-position block working to Northam Junction and also Southampton Central. Note, as would be expected, 'Train on Line' for the down line is shown on both the relevant instruments. This is one of the few views that exist of the interior of this box, which closed in 1966. From the polished condition of the lever tops, the signalmen here clearly took a pride in their job.
Tony Molyneaux – NB collection

new station at Victoria, the four lines thence to Croydon, the Quarry line and the four roads thence to Balcombe Tunnel, are his abiding memorial. His successor, Sir James Ball, was the one who enjoyed the joke most when a typist (bless her) rendered a passage in one of Finlay Scott's letters as to a derailment thus: 'As the Engineer assures me, there is nothing wrong with the permanent way. I can only conclude there must be something wrong with the Engineer.'

If anyone had told me as a youngster that flat-bottomed rail would supersede the bull-head I should have been highly sceptical. Probably the greatest advance in my time has been in the field of signalling. The whole of the LB&SC suburban area was worked by Sykes lock and block but in the country there were some curious survivals. Between East Grinstead and Horsted Keynes, the signalling was Saxby & Farmer union of lock and block where the starting signal lever had to be pulled twice, once to engage the lock and the second time to lower the signal. When I was in London (East) I discovered a track circuit in use in the Ludgate Hill area that I was assured was originally put in by grandfather Sykes in the 'eighties and for which he had to scrounge the wire. If only he had patented the device or had superimposed it on his lock and block.

I can remember when at Brambletye Level Crossing (between East Grinstead and Forest Row) it was possible to get the distant signals off with the homes on and when Burgess Hill down home signal post was 72ft high in order to be seen clear of the station buildings on the overline bridge. The first track circuit on the Brighton was through Falmer Tunnel and I have heard R. H. Houghton, the Electrical Engineer, refer to track circuits as 'nasty unreliable things'.

In the same way that the Brighton Railway was in the forefront in notching distant signal arms, so they were with the Coligny-Welch distant signal lamp which, by an arrangement of mirrors, showed a white 'V' at the side of the light – and even today a semaphore distant signal light at green cannot be distinguished as such. One practice peculiar to the Brighton was to place distant signals beneath the home signals of a terminus to indicate when 'off' that the line was clear to the stops and that there was no vehicle standing at the dead end. Those below Eastbourne Home Signals were usually facetiously referred to as 'Beachy Head Distants'. Somewhat out of context, I can remember that the signals on the Ballycastle Railway in Northern Ireland had only one spectacle – red – so that white meant all clear.

A book could be written on railway architecture from Sir William Tite's impressive block at Southampton Terminus (now scheduled as a building of historic interest and/or architectural merit) to the severely functional structures of today and one chapter should be headed 'The Railway Station in keeping', for example, the South Western Railway Tudor goods shed in red brick and Portland stone at Hampton Court built to tone in with a somewhat similar building on the other side of the river. Then there is the baronial hall booking office at Battle and (until recently) the rather absurd miniature battlements at Portchester. The overall station roof was a favourite in Victorian times and well away from the larger cities. Chichester had such a roof in the Sixties. Canterbury East retained its roof well into SR days together with the original LCDR notices in red and white and the quaint rendering 'THE way out'. Weymouth's Brunel timber roof has only recently been removed and Lymington Town's rather pathetic example remains. Mentioning Canterbury East reminds me that when I first knew it in the early Thirties, the walls were smothered from floor to roof level with a most dreadful hotchpotch of enamelled iron advertisement plates, some of them even overlapping the windows.

One of the more pleasant institutions of SR days was the Station Renovation Meeting. When a station became due for renovation and redecoration, a meeting of representatives of the various departments was held to see what additional tidying up and minor improvements could be effected, as this could be done more economically when the district engineer had his labour force at the station. The most remarkable figure at these meetings was that delightful character Ernest Barnes, (Sir) John Elliot's lieutenant, and well he went about his master's business and carried out his ideas. Barnes had an eye for line and balance and it is mainly due to him under Elliot that SR stations owed their trim and well set-out appearance when most of the other companies' stations were still in heathen darkness in this respect.

Recollections of station buildings would be incomplete without mention of that most 'over-lavatoried' station, Salisbury, built in the last days of non-corridor coaches and which had four lavatories on each of its three platforms, viz. two men's (one at each end) and two ladies' in the centre, the latter originally first and third class respectively. Another singular feature at Salisbury was a rather dismal guards' room, where the most prominent object was a Bible in a wooden case (given by some long forgotten well-wisher) and usually referred to as 'the Bible Room'. Speaking of Salisbury brings me to loudspeakers or, should we more properly say, 'the public address system'. It was in the carefree days before the war that the loudspeaker first made its appearance on station platforms. When first introduced, it was a complete novelty and directly an announcement was made all conversation stopped and everyone listened intently but nowadays no one seems to pay the slightest attention. It is also difficult to find staff with a suitable voice and some are mic-shy, as witness an

Coligney-Welch lamp on the down distant at Adversane, 26 February 1922.
E Wallis

The exterior of the station at Battle, referred to by Charles Anderson as containing a 'baronial hall booking office'. *RCH. Spence collection*

old inspector at Salisbury who could only be persuaded to say 'An'over an' Lunnon', 'An'over an' Lunnon'. Some may also remember 'The Haunted Ball Room' on the speakers at Waterloo? [On the latter Mr Anderson does not elaborate.] (Remember also the station announcer at Waterloo in the 1970s who also said 'GodLaming.)

A propos loudspeakers, I was travelling one day by the 3.30am from Waterloo to Bournemouth, which at that time had rather an intricate series of connections at Brockenhurst. At this station the announcement on the loudspeaker was (it seemed to me) not being made as intelligibly as it might have been and I suggested an alteration to the station master, who agreed with me. A week later I was travelling by the same train and heard the announcement put out in the amended form so commented favourably on it to the station master who grinned and said, 'Yes, sir, but do you know the first public reaction? On Monday morning an old lady asked me which was the train for New Milton. I replied that it was the second train at No 3 platform and asked if she hadn't heard the loudspeaker announcement, to which came the shattering reply, 'Oh, I never listen to those things – I always ask. '

Still on the same topic, the Plymouth–Brighton train then divided at Fareham, the rear portion being for Portsmouth, the front continuing along the coast to Brighton. When Percy Collins, the station master at Southampton Central announced it, he was wont to say, 'The first six coaches are for Brighton and when I say the first six, I don't mean the first two'. Another man, a comedian at Fratton, would announce, 'Now the next train is for Bristol and don't say you were told it was for Waterloo'.

Now for the trains themselves. In my early days, travelling in winter was a spartan affair. The only heating was by footwarmers, metal (often copper) containers about 2ft long by about 10in wide filled with water and acetate of soda, which were heated up in cauldrons at principal stations and damaged your shoes (or rather boots in those days) without giving any real warmth to the body. I regret to say that the Brighton was one of the last companies to provide steam heating and even Edwin Cox said he wasn't going to have it in the Isle of Wight!

Many were the misgivings by which the abolition of side-chains on passenger vehicles were accompanied. Side-chains were short, loose link couplings fixed on either side of the buffer beam between the drawbar hook and the buffers and if a train broke away, it could run for quite long distances on the side chains without necessarily parting the air brake pipe.

Many of the thirds in the Stroudley suburban block trains were open throughout, the seat backs only rising to the middle of one's back and, as boys, if we got a coach to ourselves we used to have hurdle races from end to end. Some of the SER hop-picking block trains had no quarter-lights in the end compartments of the green-house [nowadays referred to as 'bird-cage'] topped third-brakes. The Brighton ploughed a lonely furrow in the matter of Passenger, Guard and Driver communication. The standard

17

communicator was the Stroudley & Rusbridge electrical communicator, which required only one wire connection between coaches, the earth circuit being (theoretically) through the draw-gear but in practice this was usually strengthened by a separate earth-wire. The main disadvantages were that if a foreign vehicle had to be attached between engine and train, a cable had to be run round the foreigner to make communication good. However, because the passengers' alarm button was fixed where on other lines the passengers' steam heat control was located, there were constant cases of the communication being operated by passengers wishing to turn on the heating. This got so bad that latterly the electric communicator was operated by a chain fixed in the conventional position. The main advantage was that on a curved platform, for example, the guard, whose signal might otherwise be unseen by the driver, could signal on the bell. The gear came in useful for bell communication between the driver of a standard SR pull-and-push unit when in the driving end and his fireman on the engine. The fact remains that the Brighton and SR air-controlled pull-and-push gear was the only really satisfactory system. I have previously referred to the excellent Brighton time keeping in its latter days. At that time there was quite a suburban traffic between Brighton and Kemp Town and there were several passengers for Kemp Town who travelled by the 5pm City Express [it was actually called City Limited] from London Bridge due Brighton 6pm It so happened that the branch shuttle train had to leave at 6pm, so a special engine, train and men were turned out for a 6.5pm connection but night after night it ran empty as the 5pm London Bridge was in before time and the passengers caught the 6pm!

A remarkable train service achievement between the wars was the work of Archie George, Traffic, and 'Father' Dyer, Loco. By tradition, branch services radiated from Horsham but by employing pull-and-push units and making two services into one, e.g. instead of a branch train from Midhurst to Horsham and another Horsham to Three Bridges they ran one train from Midhurst to Three Bridges, avoiding innumerable engine movements at Horsham. By this means they not only gave a better service but saved seven or eight engines and managed the economy of closing Midhurst as a shed. Be it noted that the pull-and-push units consisted originally of D1 tank engines, an old six-wheeled brake (for parcels, milk, etc.) and new bogie trailer and trailer-control coach. Before we leave Archie George, we must record that in later years he was Station Master at Yeovil Junction. At that time, the West of England people were having constant trouble with their upmarket trains and scheme after scheme of improvement was tried without any real success. After watching the working, Archie suggested an alternative arrangement but was quietly snubbed for his pains. The working got so bad that in sheer desperation his scheme was tried and from that day onward there was no more trouble. But to revert to those six-wheeled brakes; years after, when the SR were dubious about propelling six-wheeled vehicles, we were able to point to the thousands of miles run by these units.

Propelling dead [dumb] buffered wagons was always frowned upon by the Board of Trade (of whom, by the way, my Father used to point out, the Archbishop of Canterbury was a member) and the Ministry of Transport but the fact remains that quite a number of privately owned dead buffered 'Vectis' wagons loaded with chalk were for many years propelled from the pits at Shide to the Cement Mills between Newport and Cowes. Incidentally, the cement company guaranteed 30,000 tons per annum to secure the rate.

One of the great attractions of the South Coast to dwellers in the North and Midlands was the ease with which it could be reached by the Sunny South Special, the through train running from Liverpool and Manchester to Brighton and Eastbourne. Then there was the short-lived Paddington–Brighton service. The intention was to provide a connection for Brighton without crossing London off incoming GWR trains but the late starts from Paddington awaiting connections caused so much damage to Brighton down business trains that the Brighton Co. soon had enough. In parentheses, it was actually necessary for the GWR to lower their track under a bridge at Westbourne Park to allow Brighton engines to pass, the Brighton loading gauge at the cornice being exceptionally high. Strange to relate, the next move was a through train to and from Brighton and the West of England via Havant and the LSWR, the precursor of the present Brighton to Plymouth. So popular were these through trains that just before the First World War a week of discussions was held between the Midland and Brighton companies with a view to a through train from the Midland system to Brighton. However, so great were the difficulties arising from inter-company rivalry, and the fact that there was no direct physical connection between the Midland and the Brighton, that the scheme had to be abandoned.

Train working cannot be dismissed without some mention of slip carriages, in the number of workings of which the Brighton was second only to the GWR. The Brighton lever slip gear was simple and robust and, whereas even with vacuum reservoirs the other companies could only apply the continuous brake once or twice, the air brake could be applied and released a dozen times. The SER used at one time to slip at Ashford in the Down direction, the Main Train going via the through line and the facing points being thrown between the portions to allow the slip carriages to run to the platform road! When this was discontinued, the slip portion came to rest on the down through line (with no platform), whereby an engine was attached in front and the slip portion was first drawn forward and then backed to the down bay. I am not sure that the remedy wasn't worse than the disease.

And now what of the men? It is difficult for the present generation to appreciate the spirit that animated the rank and file of the pre-grouping companies. A man did not work for the Brighton Railway; he was part of if and believed in it. The late Arthur Street puts it much better than ever I could in *Farmers Glory*, from which I quote, 'There is no doubt that the agricultural labourer is much better off now than he was during the period of which I am writing. He has today a higher standard of living, a broader outlook on life and a taste for amusements and interests outside agriculture but whether he is any happier or more contented is open to question. Definitely he is not such a good farm hand. I do not say this in any spirit of criticism but merely state the fact. Why should he worry about the farm after his working hours, allotted by law, are finished? But twenty-five years ago, his sole interest was the farm on which he worked. Nowadays he does what he is paid for but then he did what was right and necessary to the well-being of crops or stock irrespective of payment. Then he took a pride in his particular department of the farm and also took the responsibility of it but now he runs to the boss for instructions at every touch and turn.'

Now please read that paragraph again *mutatis mutandis* as applying to the railwayman and the railway. Let me finish this section with the tribute paid by a very fine old Station Master to one of his porters. 'He's as ready to help a poor woman with her bundles and half a dozen kids as he is a toff with his golf clubs.'

Freaks and survivals

Under this heading I am tempted to record singular features and unusual practices together with period pieces that survived from a previous age.

First of all, at the top end of the middle platform at Brighton was a glass-sided structure in which was kept a gleaming scarlet and brass steam fire engine ready to be run out on to an end-on dock in which an open carriage truck was placed ready for despatch to any place where it might be needed. Then there is the curious luggage and parcels bridge at Eastleigh where both platforms are islands and the parcels office is on the wrong side of the Salisbury loop. A short length of metal is laid at right angles to the running line and a primitive hand-propelled trolley released from the signal box is used to transfer parcels between parcels office and platform. At Brockenhurst, where a similar layout exists, there is a pivoted swing bridge across the up loop with wheels running on a quadrant-shaped track that enables platform trolleys to be moved between the up side approach road and the up platform. A propos the double island platform layout, the first public comment I heard on the fine new station layout at Hastings was, 'That's the last time I come to this station with all them steps.' At Ventnor there was no footbridge or subway; instead a ship's gangway gave access across the single track to the island platform.

Natural gas is very much to the fore at present but Heathfield station (Sussex) was for many years lit by natural gas from a lineside bore and had a small gas holder on the down side at the north end. So important was this methane gas to the Ministry of Mines that they paid for the conversion of the lighting system on the station premises to use town gas in order that the natural gas might be sent away for use by the Ministry. As the loads of freight trains grew heavier, the Brighton Co. began to realise that 10-ton goods brake vans were not sufficient, so pairs of these brakes were twinned with a most complicated gear so that the hand brake could be applied and released from either end. I regret to say they were usually referred to as the 'Dilly and Dally' brakes! Another curiosity now almost forgotten was the Necropolis Train. On the south side of Waterloo station at the back of the 'Beach' Sidings was a private station with entrance and lifts from Waterloo Road whence coffins and mourners were

Spetisbury (Somerset & Dorset line) disc and crossbar signal. *NB collection*

The Necropolis station at Waterloo as it appeared prior to WW2. *RCHS Spence collection*

Steam Bow Crossing near West Pennard, 14 August 1931. *E Wallis*

Fifty Years On
Counting down to July 2017

Andrea Durant

Anniversaries are things we sometimes approach with caution. With the passage of time, so the past seems to slip ever more into history and with it comes the risk of memories clouding.

Most of those who are regular readers of 'SW' will themselves be able to recall steam, and yet fifty years – *half a century* – ago, steam was in its final throes on what was being described as 'The last steam main line'.

No 34021 *Dartmoor* awaiting departure from Platform 10 at Waterloo with the 08,30 Weymouth train on 12 November 1966. Externally the engine is in an indescribably filthy condition yet clearly this was only 'dirt deep' and both it (and No 34018) would survive to be withdrawn at the very end, in July 1967.

Many were also out recording those times, names such as Mike Esau, John Bird, Rod Hoyle and Keith Lawrence, to mention but a few, trip off the tongue; these worthy individuals having the foresight to capture what would soon be consigned to history.

There were others too, recording the trains and the scenes and yet whose material was destined to be kept private, a personal record to be taken out and revisited on occasions and no doubt viewed with longing.

Sadly during that last half century, we can be certain that an enormous amount must also have been discarded. Well-intentioned relatives and friends, perhaps not railway minded, who on finding a box or album of 'train pictures' would cast them aside unaware of the photographic heritage they were discarding.

A powerful image of No 34018 *Axminster* seen at Nine Elms on 14 October 1966 ready for the 08.35 Waterloo–Weymouth. During the latter part of 1966, twenty of the thirty daily mainline Waterloo–Bournemouth/Weymouth services were still steam-hauled. In addition, steam had charge of a number of Basingstoke and Salisbury workings, Channel Islands services to Weymouth, all boat train specials to and from Southampton and finally the 10.35pm Southampton mail. At this time, there was another departure from Waterloo at 08.30, this being a faster Weymouth train with just five intermediate stops (Southampton Central, Bournemouth Central, Poole, Wareham and Dorchester South) taking three hours seventeen minutes for the journey. No 34018 would arrive at the same destination in four hours nineteen minutes, having made eighteen intermediate stops. By the end of 1966, the earlier 08.30 had been rostered for diesel haulage, thus making the 08.35 the first steam departure from Waterloo each day.

The Southern Way — Issue 35

Jim Seddon.

One such photographer recording the scene from 1966 on was Jim Seddon. His name is probably known to only a very few and yet, in the space of around twelve months, he left a photographic record of the end of Southern steam that must stand high among many of the better known names.

By profession, Jim worked for more than thirty years in the night telegraph office at the Post Office in London. After retirement and until his death in 1999, Jim became the editor of the *Journal of Analytical Psychology*, where he also helped with preparations for lectures and reviews. In its own obituary of him, the journal called him a 'remarkable man, an outstanding scholar and a person of widespread interests'. His friend, Andrea Durant, records some of these other interests, which included: literature; languages; the spiritual and mystical writings, ideas and philosophy of both east and west; carpentry; miniature Alpine plants; travel; steam trains; German wines; calligraphy; photography, (he had a dark room in his flat and used to print all his own photographs); and music! Obviously it is with one particular item from that list that we now concern ourselves, starting in October 1966 … .

No 34015 *Exmouth*, minus its smokebox numberplate but with nameplate(s) intact, on the first leg of the 'LCGB' 'Shakespearian' special from Waterloo to Victoria on 12 November 1966 via Feltham, Ascot, Reading, Didcot, Oxford, Banbury, Leaminton Spa, Stratford-upon-Avon, Birmingham Snow Hill, Stourbridge, Birmingham Snow Hill, Banbury, High Wycombe and Kensington Olympia. Departure was reported as one minute late from Waterloo but it was destined to be fifty-five minutes late by the time it reached Victoria. No 34015 would not survive to the end, instead it succumbed in April 1967.

No 34004 *Yeovil*, a Bournemouth-based engine and a regular and reliable performer, seen here at Waterloo awaiting departure on what was a blustery Wednesday, 16 November. The engine is again in charge of the 08.35 and waits on Platform 9. (No 35023 was at the head of the 08.30 nearby.)

On a different date *Yeovil* is seen again but this time having arrived at Waterloo and with its train released, it is seen backing down towards Nine Elms or, having been relieved of its inward service at another platform, is it now running forward (look at driver's forward-concentrated pose) to pick up ecs for Clapham Junction? It was by no means uncommon to see a Bulleid on such relatively menial duties]. The spotters – note the obligatory duffle-bags – are stood at the end of Platform 11, the longest platform at the station and an ideal vantage point for observing the comings and goings. Who and where are they now … ?

No 34060 *25 Squadron* receives attention from the driver at the end of Platform 14, having just arrived with the 11.07 from Bournemouth, 7 November 1966. With the exception of Boscombe, this service called at all stations to Brockenhurst and then ran as a semi-fast to Waterloo, being allowed three hours for the journey. Even allowing for some recovery time built into the schedule, Jim recorded the service was '14 late into Waterloo', although no reason was given.

There were no bay platforms as such at Waterloo but there were two loading bays situated between Platforms 11 and 12, mainly used by the station pilots or a main line engine awaiting its turn of duty. Here Jim recorded this image of one of the few remaining original 'Pacifics', No 34002 *Salisbury*, awaiting its next turn on a wet 28 November 1966, although the working was not stated.

Another arrival. This time No 34040 *Crewkerne*, which had been in charge of the 08.46 from Bournemouth on 25 October 1966. This was another stopping/semi-fast service, which had originated from Bournemouth West. The scheduled arrival time at Waterloo was 11.54.

Moving slightly west to Vauxhall, 'Standard 5' No 73065 on empty stock. Jim reported this as a 'dull Wednesday lunchtime', more accurately 7 December 1966.

On a dull winter's day when many photographers would have simply given up, Jim persevered and recorded No 35014 *Nederland Line* on the 13.30 Waterloo to Weymouth. Jim recounts, 'because of the weather the view was taken from under shelter and not far from the waiting room where there was a welcoming coke fire … .'

One of just two Bulleids to survive in (almost) original condition until the end, No 34102 *Lapford* is seen powering through Surbiton on the through line with the 11.30 down on 30 December 1966. This train was shown in the timetable as only going as far as Bournemouth but with a note that 'through carriages were available to Weymouth', albeit later in the day. The other surviving unrebuilt Bulleid was the now-preserved No 34023 *Blackmore Vale* on the Bluebell line.

On the same date (30 December 1966) Standard Class 5 No 73115 (formerly *King Pellinore*) passes through Surbiton on what appears to be a south-bound engineers' train. Not working for the railway and not having access to the working timetable, Jim could only comment 'No 73115 on a down goods'. In the background, the offices were those of the Winthrop computer business.

Finally on that day, Jim recorded No 34071, formerly *601 Squadron*, working hard on the up main at Surbiton, having just been checked outside the station with what he records as the 09.24 from Bournemouth. No 34071 had exactly four months left in traffic, being withdrawn on 30 April 1967 and having run 728,028 miles in nineteen years.

Further south-west to Woking on 11 October 1966, clearly a bad day for Nine Elms when it came to providing motive power for this Waterloo–Bournemouth express as all there was available was 'Standard 4' No 75075. Further details of the working were not reported.

Bulleid power at Vauxhall. No 35026 *Lamport & Holt Line* at the head of twelve coaches forming the 10.30 Waterloo to Weymouth on 22 December 1966. First stop on this service was Southampton Central and then non-stop to Bournemouth Central, where the service divided with the restaurant car terminating at that station. The white paint on the buffers had been applied on a railtour Manchester–York–Doncaster–Manchester, headed throughout by this loco a month earlier on 20 November. It would survive in service until March 1967, when it was condemned due to a loose driving wheel tyre.

In perfect autumn weather, No 34052, formerly *Lord Dowding*, passes Byfleet and New Haw 'making at least 70mph …' with the 11.30 Waterloo to Bournemouth. Such were the vagaries of the timetable that this train ran fast to Basingstoke before calling at Micheldever and Winchester. It then resumed its fast schedule as far as Brockenhurst, after which the latter part of the journey was distinctly more sedate.

On a cold 23 December 1966, No 35012 *United States Line* on the 10.30 Waterloo to Weymouth at Byfleet and New Haw. Notwithstanding the smoke deflectors, steam can be seen gathered around the top curve of the smokebox, which was common to all the rebuilt engines.

No mistaking the down *Bournemouth Belle* at the same location, recorded on 21 October 1966. We see No 34102 *Lapford* again and with a small portion of the casing not having been secured above the left-hand cylinder. At the time, *Lapford* had run for six months from its last 'Light Casual' overhaul and was also a regular performer on another named train, the rerouted Pines Express.

Fifty years on

Regrettably Jim failed to record the engine number here, although we can at least identify the type as a 'BR Standard 4'. The location is Woking on 14 October 1966 and running light engine.

Concluding this first instalment, we return to Waterloo to witness the imminent departure of the 13.30 Weymouth train behind No 34019 *Bideford* on 30 November 1966. Alongside is a Southern Railway 4COR EMU No 3131 on a Portsmouth working. The engine is clearly ready to depart, although Jim recorded that it was a further three minutes before the platform starter turned green.

Orpington/Bromley North installation. The Woodside–Selsdon branch had been closed on 15 March 1915 as a wartime economy measure, perhaps even then an indication of the sparse use made of it. But the Southern reopened it with electric traction on 30 September 1935. Stated as being for operational reasons, the third rail was extended by one station further on the Oxted line, to Sanderstead, though the route to East Grinstead remained steam-worked for another fifty years. However, the residents of that affluent, growing and, indeed, influential outer suburb had for some time been complaining about the inadequacy of the Oxted line service. Extending the Mid-Kent electrification this far may have been considered by the Southern authorities as answering that complaint. Usage would suggest it didn't!

The Mid-Kent junction with the North Kent line towards Blackheath is a few chains north of Lewisham station, itself 6 miles and four chains from Charing Cross. The Lewisham Crossover Junction takes the form of a double scissors crossing where four routes meet and divide. Those approaching at the London end are from St Johns and the mainline into London Bridge and from Nunhead on the former LCDR Greenwich Park branch from Victoria. The latter arrives on a steeply graded causeway built by the Southern Railway in 1929. This was part of an alternative route for Hither Green freight traffic to/from companies north of the Thames that had previously gained the ex-LCDR line to Snow Hill and the Widened Lines via Metropolitan Junction and Blackfriars. This move resulted from the great increase in line occupancy into London Bridge following electrification, which made freight train pathing to and through that station difficult. Resignalling with colour-lights through the south eastern suburbs out of London Bridge at the end of June 1929 saw the Lewisham area controlled from three boxes, at St Johns, Parks Bridge Junction and Court Hill Road.

The Mid-Kent passes through Lewisham station on a curve sharp enough to be check-railed, entering the valley of the River Ravensbourne, which spills into the Thames at Deptford Creek. At the end of the curve, which is on a viaduct through the station itself and an embankment for part of the way afterwards, the line is heading just west of south as it passes Courthill Loop North junction. This was also part of the 1929 freight traffic rerouting, the double track Courthill Loop providing direct access to/from the main line, Hither Green marshalling yards being a mile beyond its south junction. Hither Green loco shed was not opened until 1933, in part due to the nature of its location, which required much piling to make a solid foundation.

Having then bridged the Ravensbourne for the second time and passed beneath the four-track main line out of Charing Cross, the Mid-Kent is joined by another double track spur sweeping in on the up side. This is the Ladywell Loop, opened in 1866 from Parks Bridge Junction on the 'new' main line from St Johns to Tonbridge (see SW21). Ladywell station follows at 6¾ miles from Charing Cross though thirteen chains less if the Ladywell Loop is used and Lewisham thus avoided.

The station opened with the line, the single-storey, yellow London brick building being on the up side. Its forecourt, named Railway Terrace, is off Ladywell Road, which bridges the line at the up end. The building is the original but now devoid of almost all its chimneys and, while in good condition, much of it is unused. The down side, which has only a small shelter, backs on to a public open space named Ladywell Fields and the rear of Lewisham University Hospital. The roofed footbridge at the up end and the generous platform canopies date from SECR days. Incidentally, the locality's name emanates from a well once in the grounds of the local church of St Mary the Virgin, hence 'Our Lady's Well'.

Shortlands old and new. Electric trains had started to operate from here from 8 June 1925. *NB collection*

A little over ¼-mile from Ladywell the Ravensbourne passes under the line again to form the western boundary of a rump of Ladywell Fields on the up side. Catford Greyhound Stadium stood at the southern end of this rump, though it closed in 2003 and was later demolished after a fire. Immediately south of the stadium site the Chatham's Catford Loop, opened in July 1892 under the independent ownership of the Shortlands & Nunhead Railway, sweeps in at a higher level on the up side. It became LDCR property four years after opening. That company's Catford station stands alongside the Mid-Kent's Catford Bridge (7 miles and forty-two chains). The bridge, at the country end of the stations, carries the notorious South Circular Road, the A205, over the Ravensbourne, which flows between the two railways here. Covered steps lead down from the bridge to both Mid-Kent platforms though the presently-used building, on the down side, is on a small forecourt off Doggett Road, which has run parallel to the railway from the southern boundary of Ladywell Fields. Like Ladywell, this is single storey in London brick and faces the similarly constructed and imposing two-storey building on the up side, no longer in railway use. The South Circular dives down off the bridge to pass under the Catford Loop.

The up side goods yard, of three long sidings, did not open until the early years of the twentieth century, principally to handle domestic coal as the local area developed. There was no headshunt, the lead being directly into the up line. A long refuge siding faced it on the down side. The yard closed to general goods in March 1968, though coal traffic continued for a little longer. The small SER-style signal box originally stood at the London end of the up platform, though lengthening saw the platform engulf it. The box closed in April 1971. There was no footbridge here until 1992, this being at the up end.

Just over ¼-mile south of Catford Bridge the Catford Loop crosses over the Mid-Kent on a skew girder viaduct. And as if to emphasise the antipathy between the two companies, the loop appropriates the Ravensbourne valley to head towards Shortlands, leaving the Mid-Kent to continue its southward journey alongside a tributary, the Pool River. The Catford Loop's passing in this vicinity was accomplished only by a diversion of the Ravensbourne with compensation having to be paid to the millers affected. But the loss of their livelihood is commemorated by road names in the former London County Council housing estate to the east of the Mid-Kent, namely Fordmill, Knapmill and Grangemill.

After passing under the Catford Loop, the line describes a very elongated 'S' bend before arriving at Lower Sydenham, one chain over 9 miles from Charing Cross. This station opened in 1906 in place of the original sited slightly further north and closer to a gasworks established in March 1853 by the North Surrey Gas Company. This became the Crystal Palace District Gasworks in November that year but closed with the continued development from August 1904 of another works at a site at Bell Green, a little further north still, under the auspices of the South Suburban Gas Company. This site had been rail-connected in 1878 with a trailing outlet on to the up line. By the outbreak of the Great War approximately 150,000 tons of coal and 250,000 gallons of oil were passing over the connection annually. These totals had been reduced slightly by Nationalisation of the gas industry in 1950 when the South Eastern Gas Board took over the works. By that time, they had an internal standard-gauge railway system running to about 4½ miles worked by a number of industrial 0-4-0T engines. Following the introduction of natural gas, the works closed in April 1969, the site subsequently being cleared except for two surviving gasholders. A superstore opened on land at the south end in 1995 and further redevelopment of the rest of the site as a retail park continues though with some residential property included.

The Pool, which runs along the eastern boundary of the works site, partly in culvert, passes to the east side of the railway shortly before the line bridges the A2218 (Southend Lane) and arrives at the station. The buildings, on both sides, were of typical SER single-storey timber construction with solid and ornamental brick chimneys at the ends, the main offices being on the up side. The steel girder footbridge was to the south of the buildings and beyond the platform canopies. The station was extensively reconstructed in 1990 when new brick buildings were provided on the up side and a brick shelter on the down platform. A new steel footbridge superseded the original on roughly the same site toward the south end of the platforms.

The goods yard consisted of a single long siding on the down side to the north of the station with a goods shed alongside it a few yards off the platform end. June 1966 saw withdrawal of freight traffic. The signal box, which closed in April 1971, stood on the up side opposite the points into the siding, the usual SER timber-framed building on a brick base.

Heading due south, the outlook from a train assumes an open aspect because it passes through an area dominated by sports grounds, including the training facilities of Crystal Palace Football Club. Only a ½-mile or so from Lower Sydenham the line reaches New Beckenham. This is the second station here, the first being twelve chains further south and set within the junction between the Addiscombe and Beckenham Junction lines. It opened with the Addiscombe line in 1864. Platforms served all four roads and the main building on the up side was accessed from a forecourt off Lennard Road, which crossed the railway to the north of it. This station's layout must soon have proved unsatisfactory, for a new station opened seven chains north of the junction only two or three years later; Dendy Marshall simply dates the re-siting as '1866/7'. This station now had only two platforms with a new building on the up side.

Substantial rebuilding took place in 1904 with new brick offices on both sides of the line, though those on the upside continued to be the main one. The booking office here was renewed in 1990. Platform lengthening at the down end saw severance of the Lennard Road level crossing, by which passengers had previously passed between platforms. A subway was provided here instead for general public pedestrian use and another excavated beneath the south end of the platforms for railway passengers. For vehicular purposes Bridge Road was constructed over the site of the original station south of the junction, as its position implies passing over both railway

No 34017 *Ilfracombe* on the 'Kentish Belle' near Bickley in July 1954. This train had originally operated as the 'Thanet Belle' but was renamed by British Railways in 1951. The service operated between Victoria and Ramsgate (and return) – the original intention being to detach three cars at Faversham to service Canterbury but this was not a success and was discontinued after just one season. The service ceased to operate following the first phase of the Kent Coast electrification in 1959. *AC Cawston*

routes. Its later addition may be discerned by the steepness of the ramps leading up to the spans over the tracks. The track layout of the station now included a middle road used variously as a refuge for freight trains or to hold the pilot engine for portions to or from Beckenham Junction. The practice of splitting or joining services here ceased temporarily in 1916 but was never reinstated, the middle road being lifted in 1929.

The signal box, a large timber cabin on a brick locking room and set high at the south end of the down platform, was added at the 1904 rebuilding. The sharply curved spur to Beckenham Junction was double-track from the beginning, most trains terminating at a down side bay there, though surprisingly some worked out from quite early on over Chatham track as far as Bickley, then the limit of LCDR suburban services. Singling the spur took place in 1987, the up line becoming bi-directional. The double junction at New Beckenham remained but the down spur line was severed at the eastern end and the point-work rearranged so that it became a berthing siding in place of the one laid down in 1874 on the down side of the Addiscombe line, this then being lifted. The 1864 New Beckenham building was demolished only a few years ago, having had a long period of private occupancy: the site has since been redeveloped.

A ¼-mile beyond New Beckenham, the Mid-Kent bridges the 'Beck', a tributary of the Pool, and passes under the Chatham main line from Victoria and the WEL&CPR line from Crystal Palace, together with its adjacent Tramlink track, before immediately describing a sharp 'S' bend. Having lost the Beck, the Pool river is now in the form of the 'Chaffinch' brook, running to the east of the line and following it closely for the next ¾ mile. Until measures were taken in the 1970s to channel the Ravensbourne north of Catford, flooding of the line between Lower Sydenham and Woodside was common, with the 'Chaffinch' regularly inundating the next station, Clock House (10 miles twenty-six chains). This was a latecomer, opening in June 1890 and taking its name from a large and imposing local property that was demolished a few years afterwards.

The single-storey brick building on the Beckenham Road bridge at the north end is very typical of SER structures of the time. For example, compare Elmstead Woods and Chislehurst for style, though not for size. Similarly, the neat brick facilities and arc-roofed canopies on both platforms were also representative. The signal box, a replica of that at Lower Sydenham, stood off the south end of the up platform: it closed in August 1962. The two-road goods yard on the down side, which mainly handled domestic coal, closed in April 1965.

Having curved slightly to take up a roughly south-south-westerly direction, the line passes Bromley (originally Penge) Council's Churchfields refuse and recycling depot on the up side. This was served by a private siding put in before the Great War, with a trailing connection to the up line, though it was severed in about 1960 after several years out of use.

To be continued

Southern Camping Coaches
Part 2: 1948–1967

Mike King

The rapid reintroduction of the service by the Southern Railway was in marked contrast to the other companies and it was destined to be 1952 before their reintroduction elsewhere. However, by no means all coaches were overhauled and ready for the final year of private ownership and it was 1948 before the newly formed Southern Region of British Railways attempted a full service at or near the same levels as provided up to 1939. Theoretically, from March 1948 the stock of vehicles again stood at twenty-four and, thanks to intrepid photographer Jim Aston, who made a number of forays around the region that summer, we are able to list most sites together with the coaches at each location. Known details are as follows:

Amberley in early 1953 with ex-LCDR coaches S7 and S2 (the first BR numberings, just prefixed 'S'), ready for their final season in use. The proximity to both the goods shed and the station yard is apparent. While in this scene the sidings appear deserted, there were occasions when the pick-up goods would shunt the yard and no doubt being an enthusiast at these times would have been a distinct advantage! Maybe for others there was novelty value. The chalk pit (out of sight to right) provided a certain amount of traffic in those days – usually shunted into the station yard by their own locomotive. *Author's collection*

Southern camping coaches

The replacements at Amberley from 1954 onwards. The proximity to the end-loading dock is apparent. This is coach S30S (later BR number) – ex-Wainwright SECR composite 5319. By 1963 this was west of Salisbury and was seen at Swindon Works in January 1964. In July 1966 it was renumbered as Western Region departmental DW150382 at Cardiff, being withdrawn in October 1968. To the right is LSWR composite S31S. The plate rack in the kitchen area is clearly visible. From 1962, two Pullman cars replaced the ex-SR coaches. *Author's collection*

Location	Camping Coach No(s)	Remarks
Amberley	3, 9	By 1949 coaches were 2, 7.
Bere Ferrers	?	
Combpyne	Probably 1	New site. Definitely coach No. 1 in 1950-53.
Corfe Castle	22	
East Budleigh	6, 11	By 1949 coaches were 5, 9.
Gunnislake	?	Used in 1947, but believed not used in 1948.
Hinton Admiral	25	
Littleham	?	By 1949 coaches were 16, 26.
Lyndhurst Road	23	By 1948 coach was No. 15.
Martin Mill	?	Not sure if used in 1948. By 1949 coaches were 4, 6.
Newton Poppleford	4, 7	By 1949 coaches were 3, 11.
Otterham	5	Believed 1948 was final year.
Port Isaac Road	21	
Sandling Junction	27	
Tipton St Johns	26	New site. By 1949 coach was No. 13.
Umberleigh	2	Site not used again until 1963.
Whitstone & Bridgerule	14	New site.
Woodbury Road	20	By 1949 coach was No. 14.
Wool	15	By 1949 coach was No. 19.
Wrafton	13, 16	

At a guess, coach 10 remained in departmental use at Paddock Wood (it was still there in December 1947), nos. 18 and 19 may have been at Bere Ferrers or Littleham, while coach 24 was awaiting overhaul at Eastleigh as late as April 1948.

41

The regular coach at Combpyne from 1954 until 1963 was LSWR composite S38S (ex-5056), seen on site on 18 September 1961. The livery is green with 'Camping Coach' in off-white and the number in the usual Gill Sans yellow. Note that the roof ventilators have been sheeted over – probably to keep out the rain. This coach was withdrawn in September 1968, probably after a period in departmental use. Nos. 31 and 34 were identical. *AE West*

The above largely reflects the sites perpetuated under British Railways, although Gunnislake, Otterham, Port Isaac Road and Umberleigh were soon dropped, while Sway replaced Whitstone & Bridgerule from 1958. Woodbury Road was renamed Exton in September 1958. Several stations proved more popular than others and there was an increasing trend to provide more coaches at these locations – Littleham and Martin Mill in particular received three or even four vehicles by the early 1960s.

In 1953 it was decided to withdraw the ten remaining type A ex-LCDR six-wheelers and to retain the status quo ten more bogie vehicles were converted ready for the 1954 season. This would also simplify the hire rates, which, with low, medium and high season, were becoming more complicated. One coach was of SECR origin, the rest LSWR. These were the last conversions of former Southern coaches. Details are as follows:

Camping Coach No.	Former Identity	Built By	Disposal Wdn
30	D304 50ft 1in compo 5319	SECR 7/07	DW150382, 7/66 10/68
31	D274A 56ft compo 5065	LSWR 12/07	At Southall, 9/68 To KESR
32	D411 56ft brake compo 6538	LSWR 11/18	DW150383, 11/66 10/78
33	D22 57ft third 704	LSWR 12/20	At Landore, 5/66 ?
34	D274A 56ft compo 5049	LSWR 2/10	To LMR 021801 8/69
35	D280 52ft compo 5108	LSWR 3/13	To LMR 021802 8/69
36	D408 56ft brake compo 6481	LSWR 2/12	To LMR, Bescot 9/83
37	D17 56ft third 622	LSWR 1/10	At Southall, 12/67 ?
38	D274A 56ft compo 5056	LSWR 6/06	At Swindon, 1964 9/68
39	D21 56ft third 673	LSWR 673	At Westbury, 9/74 To BRPS

Nos. 32, 33 and 39 were former corridor vehicles. These were outshopped by March 1954 and all survived to be taken over by the Western Region in January 1963 – being located west of Salisbury at that date. All subsequently entered some form of WR departmental stock, while the three passing to the LMR were either at Mid-Wales or West Midlands locations when the next round of regional boundary changes took place.

Southern camping coaches

The only 56ft, all-third, non-corridor coach to be converted was SR No. 622, seen as camping coach S37S at Newton Poppleford on 20 September 1961, with brake composite S36S beyond. Notice the proximity to the running line – here the advertised provision of an alarm clock would probably not be necessary – this function being provided by the 7am Exmouth–Tipton St Johns train, due at 7.21! *AE West*

Nos. 30 and 31 replaced ex-LCDR coaches 2 and 7 at Amberley, 32 and 33 went to Martin Mill, while the rest took up locations in Dorset and Devon. It became more common for vehicles to return to the same sites year on year during the 1950s–60s; for example coach 38 became the regular at Combpyne from 1954 until 1963, when this site ceased to be used – no doubt because the station had become unstaffed. As track rationalisation took place, some coaches became marooned on isolated lengths of track, making winter visits to workshops more difficult – and eventually impossible from some locations. This was more often the case post-1960 and became apparent from the declining external appearance of some coaches. The service was now starting to lose its appeal and the popular press began to lampoon it. The author recalls a newspaper cartoon showing a less-than-happy wife standing in front of a coach while her husband (looking rather more pleased) stands by. The caption read, 'And to think you promised me Capri this year!'

The regular 1950s sites for the twenty-four SR coaches were as follows, with the 1960 allocation shown in brackets, by which time five Pullmans were available:-

Amberley	2 coaches (30, 31)	Newton Poppleford	2 coaches (36, 37)
Bere Ferrers	2 coaches (19, 25)	Sandling for Hythe	(P40/41 from 1960)
Combpyne	(38)	Sway (from 1958)	(20, 21 from 1960)
Corfe Castle	(P43 from 1960)	Tipton St Johns	(13)
East Budleigh	2 coaches (34, 35)	Whitstone & Bridgerule	(until 1957) (–)
Hinton Admiral	(24)	Woodbury Road/Exton	(14)
Littleham	2 coaches* (16, 23, 26, 27)	Wool	2 coaches (P42/44)
Lyndhurst Road	(15)	Wrafton	2 coaches (18, 22)
Martin Mill	2 coaches* (32, 33, 39)		

*Littleham increased from two to four coaches in 1960, Martin Mill from two to three.

56ft brake composite 6481, as coach W36S, at Swindon in February 1964 along with W37S behind and surrounded by chocolate and cream painted ex-GWR campers. Most of the ten ex-SR coaches were re-varnished at Swindon prior to their final summer of use in 1964. Note the provision of an external handbrake lever, standard for all camping coaches. By 1967, the coach had passed to the London Midland Region and was at Birmingham Moor Street station. It later moved to the site of Bescot loco shed, finally being scrapped in September 1983, by which time it was on an isolated section of track and looked pretty disgraceful. However, it retained faded Southern Region green livery and insignia to the end. *PH Swift*

Corridor composite 5108, now W35S at Birmingham Moor Street on 29 April 1967, In company with vehicles 34 and 36. This coach (and No. 34) later entered LMR internal user stock as their 021802 and 021801 respectively and were both withdrawn in August 1969, being seen outside Wolverton Carriage Works a month later. Both were broken up in March 1970. *PH Swift*

Southern camping coaches

High-roof corridor brake composite W32S at Swindon in March 1964. This coach served at Martin Mill (Kent) from 1954 until 1961, then moved westwards to Wrafton before passing to the Western Region in January 1963. It later became departmental DW150383 at Worcester in November 1966, finally being withdrawn in October 1978. *PH Swift*

'Smartie's coach' – ex-SECR Royal saloon 7930, now as Scottish Region camping coach SC51, labelled (not strictly accurately) 'Pullman Camping Coach' and in light blue livery at Glenfinnan on 21 August 1967. One wonders if marketing it as a former Royal vehicle might have had some value. It would last just two more years and was destined to be the last ex-SR camping coach in use. A true Pullman camper stands behind. *JH Aston*

Post–1960 developments

The service clearly needed some fresh thinking if it was to survive into the more affluent 1960s and the short-term answer came in the form of redundant Pullman Cars. The first conversions used the cars withdrawn from the Kentish Belle, which had ceased running on completion of phase one of the Kent Coast electrification in June 1959. Eight of the former LNWR-underframed 'J' class cars and the sole surviving 'T' class car (on an ex-GWR underframe) were converted in time for the 1960 season. Five were retained by the Southern; going to Corfe Castle, Sandling (two) and Wool (two); three others went to the London Midland and one to the Scottish Region. The SR allocation was numbered from 40 upwards, prefixed 'P' to denote their Pullman origins.

This allowed the redeployment of some ex-Southern coaches and the early withdrawal of some of the pre-war conversions. As might be expected, these were marketed as 'Luxury Pullman Camping Coaches' and commanded higher weekly rates, although they still catered for six persons, just like all the SR conversions. They were also all-electric but the lavatory facilities remained available only within the station premises! However, it is believed that an Elsan toilet was later provided for night-time convenience.

Further Pullman conversions followed using some ex-SECR eight-wheeled 'G' class and twelve-wheeled 'H' class vehicles, with several done for the Eastern and the Scottish Regions as well. Those on the Southern (and the three LMR coaches) retained Pullman umber and cream livery but those on the ER and ScR carried a rather attractive blue colour. As these were received by the Southern, there was a reallocation of older vehicles and many of the former Southern Railway coaches migrated westwards – which is how all ten of the 1954 conversions passed into Western Region hands in 1963 – destined to last until the end of September 1964. Several Pullmans were also in the west but some of these were reclaimed by the Southern Region to give a few more years' service. The 1961 edition of the British Railways camping coach holiday brochure lists all 134 sites nationally, including the usual sixteen SR locations. These were described as either inland or coastal – all the SR sites were judged inland. By now these were:-

Amberley	2 SR coaches	Lyndhurst Road	1 Pullman car
Bere Ferrers	2 SR coaches	Martin Mill	3 SR coaches
Combpyne	1 SR coach	Newton Poppleford	2 SR coaches
Corfe Castle	1 Pullman car	Sandling for Hythe	2 Pullman cars
East Budleigh	2 SR coaches	Sway	2 SR coaches
Exton	1 Pullman car	Tipton St Johns	1 Pullman car
Hinton Admiral	1 Pullman car	Wool	2 Pullman cars
Littleham	4 SR coaches	Wrafton	2 Pullman cars

The first SR Pullman camping coaches were ready for service in 1960. This is P41 (ex-'J' class brake third either No. 15 or 16) with P40 (similar brake No. 11) behind at Sandling for Hythe when first converted. Sandling had ceased to be a junction when the Hythe branch closed on 3 December 1951. The coaches are standing on a siding adjacent to the former branch platforms – the main line platforms are behind the building at the rear and the footbridge leading to the down main platform may just be seen. The two end shutters could be opened to provide a veranda and additional ventilation. Coach P51 (formerly *Sapphire*) was later transferred here from Bosham and by 1971 was the only Pullman remaining on site – albeit somewhat derelict.
Author's collection

Notice that the number of coaches was now twenty-nine – more than at any other time. Rates varied from £6 to £10-10-0d (£10.50) per week for the standard coaches and from 9 guineas (£9.45) to 15 guineas (£15.75) for the Pullman cars, depending on season, which ran from mid-March to Mid-October. The cost of heating, lighting and cooking would need to be added to these

Southern camping coaches

figures while the usual travel arrangements and adult fare purchases from the home station still applied. Further Pullman car conversions followed during 1962 and 1963, bringing the SR total up to 25 (coach numbers P40-P64) while others were added to the ER and ScR totals, bringing their numbers up to 11 each, together with six final ones for the Western Region – but more of these anon. The number of former Southern coaches continued to decline as they were replaced by Pullman cars and just the ten 1954 conversions remained into 1962. The last location changes now took place, Bosham being new for 1962, Yalding, Birchington-on-Sea, Walmer and Umberleigh being added in 1963 – the latter not having seen a camping coach since 1948. The car at Umberleigh was a former SR vehicle, No. 33. Since Combpyne was no longer used, the Western Region then had one spare ex-SR vehicle. This was replaced by a GWR eight-berth coach for the final season in 1964.

Twelve-wheeled ex-SECR car P48 (previously third class No. 96 and, before that, first class car *Sylvia*, dating from 1921) at Tipton St Johns on 8 September 1961. 'Holiday Coach' was the usual description applied to SR Pullman campers and the former Pullman lettering and crest was retained – clearly regarded as favourable advertisements in their own right. *AE West*

Details of the Pullman car conversions for the Southern are as follows:

Camping Coach No.	Class	Former Identity*	Date	Converted Known location(s)
P40	J	Third class No. 11	3/60	Sandling for Hythe
P41	J	Third class No. 15*	3/60	Sandling for Hythe
P42	J	Third class No. 16*	3/60	Wool
P43	J	First class *Coral*	4/60	Corfe Castle
P44	T	Third class No. 30	4/60	Wool
P45	G	First class *Ruby*	3/61	Lyndhurst Road
P46	H	First class *Hibernia*	3/61	Hinton Admiral, later Lyndhurst Road
P47	H	First class *Rosalind*	3/61	Exton
P48	H	Third class No. 96 (ex-*Sylvia*)	3/61	Tipton St Johns

47

Camping Coach No.	Class	Former Identity*	Date	Converted Known location(s)
P49	G	First class *Seville**	4/61	Wrafton, later Yalding
P50	H	Third class No. 45*	4/61	Wrafton, later Walmer
P51	G	First class *Sapphire*	4/61	Bosham, later Sandling
P52	H	Third class No. 98 (ex-*Milan*)	5/61	Corfe Castle
P53	G	First class *Valencia**	5/61	Exton
P54	G	First class *Florence**	11/61	Amberley
P55	G	First class *Regina*	11/61	Amberley
P56	H	Third class No. 8	1/62	Littleham, later Birchington-on-Sea
P57	H	Third class No. 6	1/62	Littleham, later Birchington-on-Sea
P58	G	First class *Hawthorn*	1/62	Littleham
P59	H	Third class No. 99 (ex-*Padua*)	3/62	Littleham
P60	G	First class *Daphne*	3/62	Sway
P61	G	First class *Leghorn*	3/62	Sway
P62	G	First class *Sorrento**	4/62	Martin Mill
P63	G	First class *Corunna**	4/62	Martin Mill
P64	G	First class *Palermo*	4/62	Martin Mill

* The former identities of some cars are in some doubt. Some sources consulted show P41 and P42 transposed, P49 to be ex-*Rainbow*/*Cosmo Bonsor*, P50 to be car 47 and P53 and P54 transposed. It has not been possible to verify which are correct. See individual photo captions for more details.

Cars sent to the Eastern region were numbered CC161–171, those to the Scottish Region were SC40–51, while the three LMR cars were numbered in their internal user series as 022260–62.

The six on the Western Region were numbered W9869–74 in their camping coach series.

Conversions were done at the Pullman car works at Preston Park but the vehicles were sent to Eastleigh for final equipping and some other repairs. Relevant orders for these were E4750 for cars P40–44, E4949 for cars P45–53, E5071, 5123 and 5131 for cars P54–64.

Car P53 at Exmouth on 2 June 1965. This was formerly *Valencia* or *Florence* – depending on which source is consulted as cars 53 and 54 are often shown transposed. As both were externally similar, the author is unable to confirm which identity is correct. By 1965 all Western Region camping coaches had been withdrawn and the vehicle is at the end of a line of eight in Exmouth goods yard, awaiting removal for scrapping or transfer to departmental use. The others in the line were P47, P58, P59 and W34–37S inclusive – from Exton, Littleham, East Budleigh and Newton Poppleford. *AE West*

Southern camping coaches

From 1965 the Southern Region had just twenty Pullmans spread over ten sites and this would remain until the end of the 1967 season. Coach P60 (ex-*Daphne*, built for SECR services by BRCW in 1914) is at Sway together with car P61 (ex-*Leghorn*) behind, on 3 August 1965. *AE West*

Various cars were exhibited at Waterloo, Victoria, Southampton and possibly elsewhere during the winter periods of both 1960 and 1961, to help publicise the service.

Despite all this effort, the service was not destined to last much longer. The Beeching report would inevitably have an effect on camping coaches as many of the lines on which they were situated were being proposed for closure, while at best the stations on lines remaining open were to become unstaffed. Either way, the necessary support services to maintain the coaches would soon disappear, consigning the scheme to history. A BRB statement issued in January 1965 said, quite simply, 'that there will be fewer camping coach sites this year'. The Western Region had already decided to withdraw its vehicles and so most of those on the East Devon branches were collected together at Exmouth for departmental redeployment, while any still in North Devon were assembled similarly at Barnstaple Junction. Some had not been returned to works for several years and were starting to look shabby. The Pullmans on the Southern Region soldiered on until 1967 – some remaining at their last station until either broken up or purchased for preservation, usually during 1968–71. By this time just twenty cars remained at the ten remaining SR locations listed above.

By the mid-1960s, the public demanded something better. Mass car ownership had dented the holiday traffic carried by the railways and the lure of cheap Continental package holidays had done the rest. The six remaining Western Region Pullman camping coaches (all ex-SR) were collected together at Marazion, Cornwall, and the eight ordinary coaches at Dawlish Warren and all were then used exclusively by the BR staff association for a number of years. While the Dawlish site received modern BR Mk 1 vehicles in the 1980s and continues to operate to this day – again for public use – the Pullmans at Marazion gradually fell into disuse until they became so decrepit that they were considered a local eyesore. Two were saved and purchased for preservation as part of a hotel at Petworth station in Sussex, where they now cater for a very much more up-market clientele, but at least three were finally demolished under an order from the Penzance local authority in 2003. However, camping coach holidays have seen a small revival and, using tastefully restored vintage stock, may now be enjoyed again, but in a rather different league to that provided by the railway companies half a century ago.

Rebuilt
The letters and comments pages

We have an absolute plethora of mail for this issue, so (and in no particular order) straight in with the first – from Richard Simmons:

'Kevin, I was very sorry to read in *SW31* of your health issue and trust that by now you have very much improved. [I have received many kind comments and it is appreciated. Perhaps best to say 'getting there'.]

'This is to let you know that following your plea in *SW28* for information on the Brockenhurst school trains, I am currently working on an article on this subject. [My original note was not a deliberate hint but it is most welcome. We know Richard's articles are always well-detailed and I promise it will be included as soon as it is available.] I have recently received *SW33* and as the east of Southampton is my ex-home patch I trust a few comments on Part 1 of the Southern Region colour feature will be acceptable.

No chance of getting the location of this one wrong! Wimbledon flyover with a 4SUB (headcode 61) on a down Kingston 'roundabout' service, on 20 November 1951. Climbing to Durnsford Road Power Station is 4SUB No.4153 on an up service to Waterloo.

'Page 75 – for a quite considerable time No 30707 was the regular engine used on the 10.57am Salisbury–Portsmouth & Southsea parcels from Southampton Terminus, where the train reversed. So I suggest it is not a service bound for the Western Region as suggested.

'Page 77 – upper picture. The three disc headcode carried by the engine is the same as that carried by the loco on the lower picture on the previous page, this being the Brighton–Salisbury headcode. The train must therefore be the through train from Brighton to either Cardiff or Plymouth and not Portsmouth although, of course, it did carry a portion from Portsmouth [Attached at Fareham]. Maybe that is a bit pedantic [Be assured – not at all].

'Page 79 – lower picture of the main station building at Woolston. The recently built tower blocks referred to in the background are definitely not part of Weston housing estate, that estate being approximately a mile away roughly behind the photographer. The buildings depicted are on Defender Road, developed in the 1950s and replacing housing destroyed in the Second World War along with the nearby (also destroyed) Supermarine factory – which produced the famous Spitfire fighter planes.

'Page 80 – lower picture. No 30707 again on what must be the 10.57 Salisbury parcels. Station time, (I loathe the term 'dwell time') at Netley in the 1960 Working Timetable is 1.21pm to 1.42pm: twenty-one minutes to unload parcels and clear the down line for the 12.42pm Salisbury-Portsmouth DEMU to overtake. The latter departed Netley at 1.37pm. But it also had to leave the up line clear for the 1.03pm Portsmouth & Southsea-Salisbury DEMU, whose station time at Netley was 1.33½ to –1.34½, so it must have had to have shunted to the yard, which was on the up side, and the uppermost picture on the same page seems to depict such a move. So 30707 must have been on its way to the yard or just come out.

'Page 81 – upper picture. After No 30707 had finished its exploits on this particular van train it was replaced by 'Dl' No 31735, which also worked the train quite regularly for a time. In the caption the number 31725 is an error as 31725 was a class 'C'.'

Richard, thank you. He also speaks of an article on something else very local that we will be contacting him over very shortly … !

Now from John Lacey:

'Another great issue, No 33. I was a bit surprised though that the picture on page 6 could not be identified as to location. Looking at the lever leads, most of which are clear, there can only be one location, which is where lines from West Norwood and Tulse Hill meet – Leigham Junction. It is indeed Leigham Junction as it was before the rebuilding in October 1951. If any of your readers know, I would like to discover what type of frame was installed in 1951 to replace the Saxby one depicted?'

If anyone has any thought do please pass them on. We have both checked in the SRS 'Signal Box Register' but there is an omission in what is normally a superb source for reference as there is not even a mention of the 1951 rebuild.

Our friend Jim Gosden comments on the 'T14' type ('Paddleboxes') following Jeremy Clarke's recent article and also on the smoke-deflectors, which I suspect will start a new thread of conversation… .

'I have fond memories from my youth of the T14s in their much rebuilt form from 1943 to their demise in 1951. One could stand on Walton-on-Thames station and hear a T14 approaching on a down Basingstoke semi-fast from as far away as Hersham station and even beyond. I am sure they were driven on 50 per cent cut-off from the glorious sound they made.

'And from one conundrum to another – smoke deflectors. I have long found it intriguing, if not puzzling, that of the 'Big Four' railways from 1923 to 1939, the Southern had more classes of locomotives with smoke deflectors than the other three.

'The GWR had none of course. Likewise the LNER had none until *Cock o' the North* and *Earl Marischal* came along. The LMS only had the original Royal Scots and Patriots, with their big parallel boilers, and the odd Claughton. By contrast, the Southern seemed to put deflectors on almost everything! Lord Nelson and Schools understandably, but the N15, S15, H15, even smaller types, U, U1, N and N1, The 2-cylinder Moguls are perhaps the most puzzling of all, for were they not a Maunsell (Holcroft) variant of the GWR 43xx? Whatever, 366 engines in total from ten different classes.

'What is puzzling is that tank engine classes derived from the same tender engine versions were not fitted. Is there any documentary evidence that supports the fitting of deflectors to so many locos? Perhaps it was simply down to aesthetics or fashion, after all the French seemed to nail them on to almost everything – including tank engines!'

'Maybe someone has already done some research on the subject which could then appear as an article in *SW*?'

Jim's words not mine, but I wholeheartedly agree that it would be of great interest. Jim's questions came by letter –

One thing that comes up as a puzzle every so often is how (and when) did outlying depots send their engines to main works for overhaul/repair? With a 'main-line' engine this was easy, simply use it to work (or even double-head) a train in the requisite direction, no doubt returning in like fashion after a suitable running-in; but what of the smaller tank engines, did they too work a service? Although, what duty might, say, a 'B4' be used for, if venturing from Plymouth to Eastleigh? Possibly one answer would be 'dead' haulage with rods removed but under these circumstances, speed would need to be restricted as the driving wheels would no longer be in balance. The conclusion reached is that small tank engines, whether in steam or under tow, were moved at night, when line occupancy was less and a small engine moving at perhaps 20mph would cause minimal disruption. No doubt the same was true in the reverse, movement at night – except here – where the camera has recorded former PDSWJR 0-6-2T No 757 *Earl of Mount Edgcumbe*, seemingly fresh from overhaul, passing Axminster and heading west. No date is given, and no, we did not include it as an example of a tank engine type that might benefit from smoke deflectors as per Jim Gosden's letter!

yes we still welcome these but PLEASE note the PO Box is now defunct so do use the home address, details of which are at the start of this issue.

My personal response to the topic was as follows: I suspect the use of smoke deflectors on the Southern was an attempt, let us be honest and say not always successful, at getting the smoke to rise clear of the driver's view. I recall talking to a retired engineer only a couple of months ago and he commented that experimentation with steam was very much a hit and miss affair, more hammer and chisel rather than technology. That said, GWR engines also had a smaller blast pipe, thereby creating a greater draught but I do agree with you 100 per cent; why should it be deemed so necessary on the SR and not the LNER? So far as tank engines were concerned, I suspect this was because of the lower speed likely to be involved.

We move away (temporarily) from *SW* now and go instead to the paperback I produced with my friend Hugh Abbinnett a few years ago on the topics of the SR DEMUs. I always envisaged *SW* as being a vehicle for additional material on previously published Southern matters – regardless of publisher – so I had better abide by the same statement! This is from Chris Sayers-Leavy:

'I recently read through a copy of your SR DEMU booklet and I think that I can answer a question that you posed in the text of the book – and make some other comments that you might find interesting … although I now notice that this message has rather turned into a 'tome' I'm afraid … .'

'You ask the question on Page 6 of the book (centre column) as to 'why the available carriage underframes that were laid down as replacement loco-hauled coaching stock for the Hastings route were shorter than normal?' Well, it has always been my understanding that the overriding governing factor was the length of the platforms at Cannon Street station. Cannon Street was, after all, the SER's mainline terminus for the City of London and the banking and insurances businesses located there.

'Cannon Street, being a fairly early station, was limited to its original platform lengths, with little opportunity to develop/extend the length as they were hemmed in between the hotel building at the front and (as it is 'perched' on arches that are just on the north-side embankment of the Thames) the station 'throat', that is itself 'contained' in the area between the front of the station and the river bridge.

'I was told many years ago by someone who worked in the Southern region rolling stock design office that the length of the Hastings coaching stock was determined by taking the length of a 4-4-0 loco off the length of the platforms that were to be used and then dividing up the available length into individual carriage units. Thus the original 6S units were originally built on short underframes. This can be seen in the pictures in your book on pages 12 (top) and 20 (top) where the available 'free space' in the platforms – is about the length of a 4-4-0 loco and tender. [One of the images – 'page 12 – top' is shown again here – KR]

'Once the 6S units 'proved' the case for the DEMU operation of the 'route' so to speak, the calculation for the next batch of units no longer required the length of the loco to be taken into account, hence the underframes for the next batch could be that much longer than the 6S stock. I don't know for certain but I would suggest that the platform length at Cannon Street may even have been instrumental in the decision to build the 'Schools' class as 4-4-0s, when the 4-4-0 format was, at the time they were built, somewhat 'out-dated' and seen by some as a backward step in loco design.

The photo referred to by Chris Sayers-Leavy. 'Hastings' DEMU No 1003 is brand new at Cannon Street and attracting attention. One can almost imagine the comments/thoughts of some of the old railwaymen present, 'It wasn't like that in my day … what will they come up with next?' Looking at the view carefully it also appears to be temporarily formed of just five vehicles. *Arthur Taylor*

'All of the forgoing may of course be old news to you now? I'm not that well read in terms of railway books and the above information may well have been covered in detail elsewhere by other authors?

'You also mention in your text, the post-accident testing of Hastings units on the ECML following the Hither Green derailment but you stopped short of making any other comment.

'I can well remember reading a report of the testing * and I was surprised that you did not mention that, despite some criticism of the SR DEMU design, with its heavy leading/trailing bogie loads, that the units rode very well on the ECML and that there was little, if any, contribution to the accident caused by the design**. The accident was formally attributed to a broken rail and the local Permanent Way Maintenance Engineer (PWME) was dismissed as a result of the accident investigation. This was very much the accepted process of the Civil Engineering Department at the time, which was very different to all the other railway departments. Where people were found to be responsible for an incident they were often just moved sideways or, in extreme cases, promoted 'out of the way' after the investigation. The PWMEs were, after all, personally responsible for their route section, its inspection (in person) of sign off of line speeds, the maintenance and repair and the imposition of any necessary speed restrictions, which were the only 'real' risk control measure that they had available to them.

* Report extract: 'Regarding the riding qualities of the Hastings line rolling stock, the test run on the East Coast main line of the Eastern Region by a random unit, not specially prepared, that had run 50,000 miles since its last overhaul, indicated that the ride was, from the accepted classification … better than "satisfactory"; for stock designed and built over ten years ago I consider that this is creditable. I was in the train and found that the ride was comfortable and reading was easy. The riding of this stock on the Southern Region was not so good, from the comfort point of view, and the reason for this is the reaction of the bogies, which are specially designed for these trains and other electric multiple-unit trains to meet clearance difficulties on the Region, to unfavourable track conditions … From the safety point of view, however, the riding qualities are well within the acceptable limits.' Extract from paragraph 163 of the Ministry of Transport report into the Hither Green accident of 5 November 1967.

'** I believe that this was also the case with the River class locos following the Sevenoaks derailment and indeed the Metropolitan Railway continued to use the same design for a number of years but, of course, their operations would probably have been at lower running speeds. Nevertheless, it was found to be the poorly laid and maintained track that was the cause of the incident. This does not mean that large tank locos were not susceptible to riding problems. What I find interesting is that some locos were more susceptible than others. The 'Brighton' Baltic tanks had a lot of problems with 'rolling' at speed, which was put down to water in the side tanks moving from one side of the engine to the other and not cured simply by putting baffles in the side tanks. Whereas I am unaware that the GWR had any such problems with any of their 'big' tank engines running at speed.

'Unless you have actually ridden on the footplate of a steam loco pulling a heavy load, you have no appreciation of the 'forces' that are set up by the loco's traction efforts and the considerable weight that is being moved about! Add speed to this equation and you begin to wonder sometimes just how they stayed on the track!

'Now some comments on some of the other DEMUs. I well recall the introduction of the 'Oxted' units in 1962 and all the furore that there was about how cold and draughty they were. You make a passing reference in your book about the '6TC' used on the Uckfield line. I'm not completely sure that I know what you are referring to here, but there was a rake of 3 × 2BIL units and a class 33 loco that was deployed to improve passenger comfort during the winter of 1962–63. I used to see the train running as an ECS out of London Bridge at the end of the morning peak. I even wrote to the old Press & Publicity Department at Waterloo about the purpose of this formation and got a short reply back from them. My understanding was that it was a 'stop gap' formation, being used to improve certain peak services. I was not aware that it was a TC unit at all as it appeared to be just a rake of old EMUs being towed around by a class 33 loco***. I also believe that the first Oxted units had then been temporarily withdrawn while some draught prevention improvements were carried out. Clearly there was no more power available from the engine in the DEMU for improved heating, so instead they installed the vertical 'door length' aluminium draught deflectors that latterly became a regular fitting on the VEPs and also improved the door sealing by putting draught excluders made out of 'folded' Moquette in the door jambs.

'***Thinking again about this. I am far from clear how this train was organised. From memory there were no shoes on the 2BILs and I only ever saw the rake being towed – for obvious reasons (screw couplings) never propelled. So I do not believe that the 'assembly' could truly be called a 'TC' (Through Control) train. The 2BILs (again from memory) were, I think, straight Westinghouse single pipe-braked and to be used as a 'TC' unit the braking would have needed to be 'EP braked'. However, on the Westinghouse straight air brake system, the 2BIL brakes could have been fed and operated from the loco just using the air brake pipe connection from the loco but there would be a significant 'propagation' delay – shades of why they stopped running twelve-car early build 4SUBs in the 1950s – and why, of course, the 'EP' control of the air brake was developed in the first place. Then there is the matter of how the lighting and heating was catered for … So all in all the '6-TC' you referred to remains a bit of a mystery.

'This brings me on to the available 'power' in the Oxted units. What was most noticeable was that on the 'long grind' up to Upper Warlingham and Woldingham (southbound services) the carriage heating would often be shut off. You could hear the electric resistance heaters 'clicking' as they warmed up or cooled down. I don't know whether this was 'official practice' but as passengers it seemed to us that the driver was trying to squeeze as much traction power out of the engine that he could! Once the climb was over, they would run freely down to Oxted – and we could then feel the warmth again.

Not quite Oxted, but close by – the 'Cuckoo' line. BR Class 4 No 80089 at Mayfield on the 09.00 ex-Eastbourne to Tunbridge Wells on 6 May 1965. Don't forget that our own book on the 'Cuckoo' line with lots of new images, will be available shortly. *NB collection*

'And lastly ... unit No 1111. What an awful refurbishment this was. When I knew it, it was working out the last of its days on the Ashford–Hastings (now known as the 'Marsh Link') service. I don't ever remember seeing it on the East Grinstead or Uckfield services. It was the most bilious and vile thing to travel in. We used to call it the 'Flying Banana'. [Remember the first single vehicle GWR railcars were dubbed in similar fashion but then due to their shape – Ed.] The bright interior colour and the very harsh fluorescent lighting, the vibration, the smell of exhaust fumes and the heating that could not be turned off, were all very nausea-inducing and wherever possible I would avoid it like the plague. This was even to the extent of letting the service No 1111 was on depart and then waiting an hour for the other unit on the route to arrive for the next return service. I'm not sure where the 'refurbishment' was carried out but it used the (by then) BR standard yellow fibreglass. This was a product available at both Eastleigh and Swindon – I know because I had some equipment guards/shields made up in the fibreglass shop at Eastleigh ... and that was the only colour it had available!

Hopefully I have not bored you too much? I may well also comment on the latest *SW* – if you can stand it!'

Chris has also kindly written on other subjects that, for the sake of allowing all to contribute, we will hold over until next time.

Now from Keith Pfrangley, the Ringwood article. Firstly, this piece should have been credited to Maurice Hopper but for some reason his name was omitted, for which I can only apologise.

Keith is a local man to Ringwood and so is ideally placed to afford some more detail on the location:

'The article on Ringwood I found very interesting. The picture of Class Q No 30541 arriving at Ringwood with the freight train is the 8.50am Poole to Eastleigh, which arrived at Ringwood at 10.43am and departed at 12.43pm. The passengers on the platform are waiting for the 10.32am Poole to Brockenhurst, which was due to arrive at Ringwood at 11.01am and depart just one minute later at 11.02am.'

Christopher Fifield has also advised that, notwithstanding what was written on the reverse of the original print, the night time images (page 94) purporting to be of Stewarts Lane should in fact be Nine Elms. At this stage I start wondering, for presumably if it was the photographer who had been confused, what else did he actually record at Stewarts Lane? We will probably never know.

Now an apology to, well all, (especially Frank Spence, Alan Moon, Jeremy Staines, Mike Townsend et al) – reminded by many and summarised by Neil Knowdlen in reference to *SW33*:

'C'mon, you can't fool me that a loco received a BR smokebox number plate prior to its withdrawal by the Southern Railway in 1946 (page 45) ... and it's definitely not an SR number plate (that would have been on cabside/bunker in earlier years) so I suspect that your "Boxhill" is an imposter. Whatever it is, it has been REBUILT with a long smokebox – so that, again, precludes "Boxhill" together with "Waddon" – and it's gained an Isle of Wight bunker extension but lost its front splasher sandboxes at some time. I reckon that narrows it down to 32650, 32677 or 32678: the first of these went for preservation at the Kent & East Sussex Railway straight out of traffic so it's unlikely to have visited Eastleigh for a full cosmetic; 32677 was one of the few late survivors that didn't make it into

Rebuilt

And speaking of 'Leader', which I know we often do, Ian Shawyer has found this image that is definitely a new one to us, No 36002 being dismantled inside Brighton Works on 30 June 1951. Readers may recall No 36002 was literally only about two days away from completion when the order to suspend work on the incomplete engines was received. At that time she only lacked cab windows and some pipe work. According to Sean Day-Lewis, 'With the lessons learnt from her older sister, she would surely have been a better engine'. No she would not. Built to the same design, she would have shown exactly the same issues. Perhaps something might have resulted if Bulleid had been successful in his attempted purchase of No 36002 and her incomplete sisters for use in Ireland but, as I have mentioned before, BR could never sanction such a move just in case he succeeded and left it with egg on its face. As it was, in her 99 per cent complete state, No 36002 was originally stored at Brighton, then towed away for store out of sight within New Cross shed, then to Bognor, again for store, before being finally returned to Brighton and the fate that awaited her. Returning to my earlier comment about such moves being made at night, it is a pity there are no photographs of Nos 36002/3 being moved in this way, unless of course you know different? *Courtesy Ian Shawyer from an image purchased on the internet containing no ownership annotation*

preservation so I think what you have there is 32678 about to go on holiday at Butlin's in Minehead.

'No A816 may be looking its (her) best on page 51 but I can't help thinking it (she) was REBUILT by Mr. Robinson ... not the Great Central guy but W. Heath Robinson! I've seen a number of these pictures before and one not particularly conspicuous modification to the front end was retained to the end of the loco's life (Many readers will know the colour photo on the Bachmann model box.) – but seems to have nothing to do with the steam heat conservation work: the running plate angle gusset ends at an angle – instead of a curve – where it meets the buffer beam and the latter is very slightly shallower than standard at this point. As I say, this doesn't seem to be related to the S.H.C. equipment in any way, so I wonder whether the loco's recent 'general repairs' included rebuilding the front end after collision damage.'

Howard Bolton also comments on one of the illustrations used in the 'Seeing Life in Black & White' article, in particular the view of the firebox of 'Leader' No 36001, when in the course of being dismantled:

'You ask, "Why take the photo"? The answer is there in the image – to show what a state it was in after just a handful of days working. If you look carefully, the shell of the box has already been cut up with oxy-acetylene, when someone has come along and said – "hang on, we need a photo of that". Hence, we can see that the thing has been carefully reassembled and is being held together by strips of steel, which have been welded over the cuts in enough places to just hold things together.

'Clearly, whoever had this done was someone in authority and also someone who thought that in years to come there might, just might, be a few souls foolish enough to be asking why it was not given a better chance to succeed? Well, there in that one photo is all the evidence needed to prove that this thing was a total engineering nonsense that should never have seen the light of day. I say that as a chartered mechanical engineer, who has been around steam in many forms since childhood.

'Now, just to correct another comment in this regard – I know a LOT about stationary steam and NO stationary steam engine was EVER fitted with sleeve valves – EVER! For good reason – they are not appropriate for this application, never were, never could be – it would take a madman to imagine otherwise.

'Don't get me going on Leader – the biggest engineering nightmare ever perpetrated in the history of railway locomotives – though driving valve gear through chains runs it close … And if you want my reasons in print – let me know!' [and Howard, from one who, as you know, has also taken an interest in 'the beast' over the years, in the form it took, I could not disagree with you – Ed.]

Arthur King, examples of whose colour photography has been seen in *SW* from time to time [more always welcome please – Ed), comments as follows:

'I received my copy of *SW33* this week and it proved to be another good read. The issue had quite a bit on the photography of the Southern and this is what I'm writing to you about.

'Seeing life in black and white' was suitably thought-provoking and demonstrates again that you cannot always believe what you see. Photo manipulation was as rife in the 1930s as it is today, although it was a much more complex affair to undertake in the time before Photoshop. Whether renumbering/renaming a locomotive for a single photo shoot or removing all background detail was considered any more ethical then than it would be now is open to question.

'Roger Holmes's 'Southern Region in Colour' was interesting – and with the promise of more to come. No doubt Roger wishes – as I do – that I'd had more film and a better camera to record those now long-lost scenes. For my sins, I expended 95 per cent of the film I had in steam days on aeroplanes and relatively little on BR(S). With reference to page 75 and the colour film stock Roger used, I'd suggest these would more accurately be listed as 'Kodachrome (ie 'Kodachrome 1'), Kodachrome II, Ektachrome and Agfacolor'.

'Keep up the good work. Editorially, *SW* is still very much the magazine it was, which is meant as a compliment; please take it that way.'

On a totally different tack, Douglas Hewitt speaks on the subject of 'Merchant Navy' class coupling rods:

'I believe that one, or more, of the miniature valve-rods on preserved *Tangmere* did fail and that the failure was attributed to poor quality metal, so the suspicion concerning wartime and post-Second World War steel appears to be well founded.

'Now the following is pure hearsay; I have never seen anything in writing … At outlying sheds, I believe bent coupling rods, presumably resulting from a bout or bouts of slipping, were straightened using a baulk of timber (old sleeper?) against the shed wall and a jack. This saved removing the rod(s)/sending same to works/an out of service loco/questions being asked/an enquiry and the added bonus of no paperwork – wonderful!

'Out there, some reactionary must know this. I guess that plain rods are less thick (wide in section), between the joints, than fluted rods and therefore less likely to suffer a permanent bend. Other possibilities are that a different grade of steel was used for the replacement plain rods – plain rods require less machining.'

Ed – As a result of Doug's comments I have spoken to both Mark Abbott and Eric Best, the former a steam inspector and the latter a fitter at Eastleigh. Eric comments he was not aware it ever happened but admitted it could indeed have taken place somewhere else – dependent upon the degree of 'bend' of course. What Eric did mention was the time a T9 working a train on the 'Spratt & Winkle' line (Andover to Romsey) bent/broke a coupling rod, resulting in the rods being taken down on both sides but the engine still completing its duty with train but now operating as a 4-2-2 single! Now there is a thought … .

Next we have a few words that I regret are non-attributable [I have no doubt missed recording the credit – Ed]:

'In *SW30* 'A History of Southampton's Railways' it states that Southampton up side buildings and tower were replaced in 1988. 'Southern Rails around Southampton' gives the date of demolition as August 1966. 'Southern Steam Sunset' has a photo dated as 8 July 1967 showing the new building under construction. [Absolutely right, we should have picked that up before going to print. Indeed, I well recall seeing the clock tower minus the faces when the up side was being rebuilt in the mid-sixties – Ed.]

And speaking of modernisation and the subsequent electrification of the Bournemouth line, following the article in issue 31 on 'The Southern Railway from Inception to Nationalisation and beyond', Alan Blackburn wonders if the 4Reps ever worked on their own? Well Robert Rhodes can confirm in the affirmative:

'The last up stopping service on Saturday from Bournemouth, the 23.12 to Eastleigh was for some time a solitary 4Rep. This would have been in the mid-1970s. Usually, it seemed, the driver would use the full power available for fast acceleration but which resulted in prolonged station stops.'

Finally for this issue, from Mike King:

'First; on page 18 (*SW33*) are two pictures of Shell/BP tank wagon A75. By a remarkable coincidence, this wagon features in Mike Rhodes colour picture on page 110 of my *Southern Rolling Stock in Colour* – just published by Crecy. [We don't mind the plug as Mike really has come up trumps with his latest book – Ed.] This was taken in 1964 and shows just one difference – the absence of the A prefix to the number.

'Next, referring to the picture on page 44 of the guard sitting in his van – this is actually a new BR Mk 1 coach and is one of a series of official photographs taken in March 1951 to illustrate the new vehicles. The crimson lake and cream livery is just visible at the left of the picture. Another view, featuring the same rather grumpy looking guard, appears in Keith Parkin's book on BR Mk 1 stock (HMRS – page 28 of the original 1991 edition).

'On page 46 Graham Buxton-Smither asks about vacuum cleaner vans. There were a number of these and some details appear in the Service Stock Registers. A few appear to have received ordinary service stock numbers (suffixed 'S') but

A propos absolutely nothing to do with 'Rebuilt' but an excuse to use what is a most interesting historic view. What we have is Waterloo East, taken from the footbridge at the north end, showing the platform and curved formation that once led round to the LSWR station but was closed in 1911. Now, to see a photograph of a movement on that connection would be interesting … . *NB collection*

others were numbered in a separate V prefixed list. Numbers V1–9 and 21–26 are detailed but whether V10–20 were allocated I do not know. Some were housed in wagons, for use in carriage sidings, others were hand trucks for use on station platforms – like the one illustrated at Victoria. Perhaps, if the editor agrees, a short article can be prepared. [yes please – Ed.]

'Now on to the Ashford 1948 photographs. Mine are all prints and vary in size and origin. Some are almost certainly copies of copies – on very thin photographic paper in many instances – so probably date from the late 1940s or early 1950s and have nothing on the reverse. Others are better quality with "Southern Railway Copyright Free" on them, with a number, prefixed 'W' – presumably for wagon. As noted elsewhere in the magazine, there were C, L and M prefixed number series – and possibly others, too.

Other pictures were taken by Topical Press Agency and others are part of the Hulton-Getty picture library. The latter are outside the scope of railway books and magazines owing to their astronomical reproduction fees. Maybe this is OK if you are picturing famous personalities, royalty or the like, but goods wagons? … Others survive at the National Railway Museum in negative form and some of these appear in the Curl Collection, again referred to on pages 85–89 of the magazine.

'The wheel tyres on many of these official pictures were picked out white – workshop staff pride most certainly but the wheels under the LBSCR open wagon are likely to be the originals. These are four-hole, not three-hole disc – a feature possibly unique to late LBSCR wheelsets. Most Brighton vehicles had axlebox journal centres set at 6ft 3in apart, unlike the more common 6ft 6in or 6ft 8in settings, rendering substitution of other wheels difficult, so these wagons were likely to retain their original fittings. It also guaranteed an early demise for many of them. The self-contained buffers on the ex-SECR wagons were standard Maunsell/Lynes fittings on wagons built at Ashford after 1915. My experience of the "Plan Arch" at Waterloo was that most items there were station, civil engineering and track views, rather than rolling stock.

'Finally, the ex-LBSCR milk van at the top of page 93 should actually be numbered 1646s, not 1648s. It was formerly traffic van No 2162 – one of eight such vans built in 1908 for milk and fish traffic – and entered departmental service in 1941. Rather surprisingly, the SR Service Stock register advises that it was returned to traffic department stock in March 1946, re-entering departmental service in 1952, although this seems a little unlikely – it was probably just moved from one departmental location to another.'

That concludes this issue of 'Rebuilt', but do please keep your comments coming and, as we mentioned at the start, we already have several pages to include in Issue No 36. So, apologies to those who have written in (Anthony Hemens, Chris Sayers-Leavy, Alan Moon, Nicholas Owen and Eric Youdon) but for no reason, other than space, are having their contributions held over.

The Salisbury Goods

Stan Watkins

In January of this year we received a note from Stan Watkins *vis-à-vis* the appearance of a 'Remembrance' at Exeter Central and, even better, it was accompanied by an image of same – see page 76, *SW34*. In responding to Stan, I very cheekily asked if he had anything else that might be suitable, which produced the following result. I think you will agree they are an excellent contribution. So, on behalf of many – thank you very much! Over to you, Stan:

'Whilst crossing the long footbridge to the west of Chichester a few days after my seventeenth birthday in 1953, drifting in from the west into the goods receiving lines was a long freight train hauled by S15 30500. The loco then uncoupled and turned on the triangle adjacent to the yard, in the course of which making hideous squealing noises on the sharp curves. It then awaited a road westward and disappeared from whence it came. At the time I was living with my parents at Bognor Regis, so to see a loco from far away Feltham was indeed a treat. Local knowledge was pretty sparse in those days – was this a special train or was it a regular working?

Opposite top: Clearly someone was short of an S15/H15 on this occasion as, instead of the usual steed, 'N15' No 30448 *Sir Tristram* has been called upon to perform. The location is near Portchester on the same train and with the Salisbury–Brighton three-disc headcode, 6 October 1956. *Stan Watkins*

Bottom: This time it is back to the more usual, 'H15' No 30335, one in the series that had a raised footplate over the cylinders, seen passing through the centre road at Havant en route for Chichester, 29 October 1955. *Stan Watkins*

En route to Chichester, 'H15' No 30333 enters Fareham on the 'Salisbury Goods', 13 October 1956. Rebuilt from an 'F13' 4-6-0 in 1924 to the form seen here, the engine had a life span of thirty-four years and was withdrawn from Salisbury in 1958. *Stan Watkins*

61

And arrived, 'S15' No 30500 entering Chichester Yard 10 April 1953.

'A clue as to the train's origin was the disc headcode fitted to the locomotive to indicate the route. Checking an old issue of my Ian Allan *ABC, Southern Region*, it showed that three discs, one below the chimney, and two above the buffer beam, one in the centre the other on the right (i.e. position no. 25), signified a train from "Brighton to Salisbury via Eastleigh" and presumably return.

'I subsequently realised that this freight train was a regular working, arriving at Chichester in the early afternoon. I made a point of seeing it if I was in the area. My photos show the "Salisbury Goods", as I called it, from 1953 to 1957. Note that after my shot of No 30500, a Feltham engine, all my subsequent photos show the train hauled by a Salisbury 4-6-0 locomotive, usually an H15 in the 30330–5 series. On leaving Chichester light engine, the locomotive seemed to take a rest at Fratton but how did it return to Salisbury? – I would very much like to know!'

Well, we hope we can provide some of the answers at least and they are to be found in the weekday 'Engine Workings'

From the same spot four years later, another 'H15', No 30331 this time and with a Urie tender, 15 February 1957.

The Salisbury Goods

'London West and Southern Divisions – Weekdays, 14th June 1954 and until further notice'.

'Feltham Duty 116 scheduled for an S15.

Leave Feltham 2.25am and work freight to Salisbury.

Thence Salisbury loco from 7am to 10.06am.

10.06am to Salisbury Milford.

Shunt to 11.05am. Then light to Salisbury East Yard.

Salisbury East Yard arrive 11.12am, depart with freight at 11.27am bound for Chichester.

Arrive Eastleigh 12.48pm. (Not shown as shunt or put-off/collect so may just have been held over waiting a path).

Depart with freight to Chichester at 1.23pm arrive 3.27pm, turn and depart light engine at 3.55pm.

Arrive Fratton loco 4.29pm, remain until 11pm.

Leave Fratton on freight, 11.30pm arrive Feltham (up-reception) 3.07am.

Loco thence to shed.

The same loco was worked by a variety of men from Feltham, Salisbury, Eastleigh, Guildford and Fratton depending upon which day of the week it was!

There was a slight variation in the timings on Monday and Saturday. On the latter day the train did not leave Salisbury until 5pm and did not call at Eastleigh.

(Referring to a slightly earlier book of loco workings – weekdays 11/9/1952 UFN, Salisbury duty No 438 is shown booked for an S15, summarised as 'Salisbury to Chichester freight via Eastleigh working back from Chichester to Fratton where the engine 'was ordered to home depot'.)

After turning on the Chichester triangle, the western arm of which is visible behind the engine (and no doubt accompanied by much squealing), 'S15' No 30823 waits to run light to Fratton, 18 May 1957. Chichester cathedral is visible in the background.

Another 'H15', No 30332 at Chichester, this time on the main line and starting its return westwards, 10 March 1956.

Recorded earlier than when we saw the same engine before, No 30331 takes a rest at Fratton loco depot in the late afternoon, more than likely after working the 'Salisbury Goods', 27 March 1954.

Finally Salisbury-based (72B) No 30452 *Sir Meliagrance* at Fratton shed, still attached to a Drummond type tender, 20 April 1957. Behind is U 'Mogul' No 31637.

A Personal 'Bucket List'
Aka – what exactly did happen to No 35004?

Happier times. In rebuilt form, No 35004 *Cunard White Star* **heads west at Battledown in August 1958.**

Kevin Robertson

When it comes to railway history, I am sure I cannot be alone in: wishing I had seen/taken more notice of/been around to ask/meet. etc, etc. Such thoughts may perhaps indicate I am just a 'sad old git' (my daughters may agree, but I am deliberately not showing them this, so they do not get the chance to comment) while I suspect there are many of us who occasionally dream of being able to go back in time and visit – or whatever.

One of those 'I wonder' thoughts is a regular consideration of mine and concerns the sub-heading for this piece, 'what exactly did happen to No 35004?'

At this point I should explain. No 35004 *Cunard White Star* had been one of the regular members of the 'Merchant Navy' class I noticed on my school trips by train between Winchester and Southampton in the 1960s. On the way home, I would also sometimes stop off at Eastleigh for a sneak visit to the sheds – I never did manage to get into the works – and it was on one of these shed visits that I became aware of this engine 'dumped' outside the front of the shed. She certainly looked a sorry sight. The tender was missing, as were the name and number plates, but what I noticed more than anything else was a piece of tyre, perhaps a foot or more long, which was broken off from the front nearside driving wheel. Either I asked or perhaps I was told by one or other of the fitters I had befriended at the shed, that the engine had been withdrawn as a result of a slip. Today I wish I had asked further for the incident itself, as well as the subsequent consequences, have often been recalled in the ensuing half century.

To return to the period in question (the winter of 1965–66), on several subsequent visits No 35004 she was still there, certainly abandoned and seemingly ignored or, as it seemed in my youthful ignorance, forgotten. That is until early 1966, when suddenly it was noticed No 35004 was being cut up on site, no doubt deemed 'unfit to travel'. I have since learned that Messrs Cohen's 'flying scrappers' undertook the dastardly deed. The remains of No 35004 were finally removed in a number of wagons that had been strategically placed alongside. At the time, it was, so it seemed, 'just another one gone', although certain aspects of her demise would continue to haunt me for years to come.

No 35004 in original form. Built at Eastleigh, the engine entered service in October 1941 and remained allocated either to Exmouth Junction or Salisbury until 1964. It was rebuilt to the form seen in the summer of 1958 and subsequently spent the final years of its life allocated to Bournemouth. The engine is seen here at what is probably Wilton, waiting to take on the 'Devon Belle'.

The problem was, for many years, my own memory. Somehow I had convinced myself that No 35004 had been dumped *facing* the front of Eastleigh shed and yet I knew from the report in the December 1965 *Railway Observer*, that she had slipped to disaster on an 'up' train. 'On 28th October 1965, 35004 *Cunard White Star* failed between Basingstoke and Hook with a broken right-hand coupling rod whilst working the 07.24 Bournemouth Central–Waterloo. Also, the left-hand rod was bent, fouling the up local line. This caused widespread dislocation of up and down services and the following up main trains were diverted via Reading General and Virginia Water, 0620 and 0725 Exeter Central–Waterloo and 0732 Weymouth–Waterloo.'

If the engine had been working north but was then towed back to Eastleigh, how, I wondered, was it that she ended up facing south? This incorrect assertion lasted until just some months ago when I happened to mention my quandary to Nigel Barnes-Evans. Totally out of the blue Nigel responded, 'I recently bought two photos at a local railway event of No 35004 after she bent her rods ... both were taken at the scene ... .' Nigel went on to apologise over the poor quality but that is of little consequence considering their historic merit.

This again got me searching and this time common sense came to the fore. I recall seeing a view credited to John Bird of No 35004 outside Eastleigh shed and, of course, she is facing north – I had been wrong all the time.

Next, it was a bit of detective work trying to put together the last weeks of life of the engine. So, we know that between 26 August and 1 October 1965, No 35004 had received a 'light-casual' repair at Eastleigh and had its life extended by a further 10,000 miles. On that basis she could have been expected to have survived longer – certainly into 1966 and perhaps even beyond. The events of 28 October were to change all that.

View the two images provided by Nigel and it is very obvious this was also no ordinary slip; might it have been caused by the engine starting to prime? Indeed it may even be that we should be fortunate the engine was not derailed or another train involved.

Correspondence then took place with Eric Youldon, who, having been shown the two views of No 35004 after she had come to rest, commented, 'No 35004 is something of a poser. The valve gear and side rods are all well and truly wrecked on both sides and probably so was the inside gear and connecting rod. You suggest the problem may have been due to water being carried over to the cylinders; this was something that could certainly create havoc but wasn't likely to result in a violent slip. I suggest a likely cause was a jammed regulator valve following heavy-handed regulator control. The wheelspin could have been brought under control by winding the reverser into backward gear but, from the position of the radius rod in one of the photographs, this was not done. The

67

The last works visit for No 35004. The engine is seen here inside Eastleigh between 26 August and 1 October 1965, wheel sets out and in the process of a 'light casual'. This was scheduled to extend its working life by a further 10,000 miles. *Ken Vernon/WRL Archive*

only people who could relate what occurred in that cab would be the engine crew concerned. The Pacific would have travelled some distance while wheelspin occurred because Basing to Hook was a stretch where they got a move on.'

Eric continues, 'I once observed, *French Line* [No 35019] at Eastleigh soon after it was rebuilt with the LH cylinder in a bad way, (I didn't check the right side.) The front cover was missing and it had wrenched out several studs, which had taken with them some chunks of cylinder casting. For certain this was a case of water (which is incompressible) being carried over, although here all rods and motion remained in order.'

Now we know that at the time of the incident there would have been other trains around and it is to the credit of the train crew that they acted promptly to safeguard other traffic. As reported earlier, Control diverted some trains via Reading, while presumably other up-Bournemouth line trains were sent via the Mid-Hants? I should also say that, despite my error of judgement over the way the engine was facing when seen at Eastleigh, I am 100 per cent certain the reference to the broken tyre I mentioned at the start is correct.

A personal 'bucket list'

The two images found by Nigel Barnes-Evans showing No 35004 after the Hook incident. Identification of what is presumably a member of the footplate crew may well reveal the answer 'how' – any suggestions would be welcome. Although of indifferent quality these two views are absolutely unique and indicate some of the forces that were involved.

The late DL Bradley reports damage to No 35004, other than to the rods, was 'minor', but he also states that this was a time when even minor repairs were no longer being authorised and the result was the engine was condemned. So, was she condemned just because of the damaged rods or was there some other damage as a consequence of the slip? Was the broken tyre the initial cause, creating the circumstances that caused the wheel to turn within the tyre? Or was it simply that, when the engine reached Eastleigh, a front-axle substitution took place to keep another of the class in service? If so, why reassemble No 35004 if she was likely to be scrapped on site – she could certainly not have travelled far in that condition. There are also other questions: what happened to her tender* – this was certainly not with her when the engine was dumped at the shed nor when she was dismantled, whilst if the broken tyre did occur at Hook, how did she arrive back?

No 35004 dumped – *and facing north* – outside the front of Eastleigh shed. The presence of the diesel shunter may indicate she was actually just being placed in that position. No doubt the 'powers' have already inspected her and reached a decision. The missing cab sheet is something that had been removed subsequent to the incident for it was certainly intact after the engine had come to rest near Hook. *John Bird/Southern Images*

69

Standard Class 5 No. 73114 *Etarre* is going well as it leans to the curve on 18 September 1960 with the diverted 07.03 Southampton Docks–Waterloo boat train. The single Mid-Hants line runs on the right, that to the left being the Meon Valley route, truncated at Farringdon since 1955. *Author's collection*

Over the Alps '60s style

Class 700 No. 30698 with the short 09.45 freight service from Ropley heads tender-first on the outskirts of Alton on 26 July 1961. Note the typical concrete p.w. hut on the left. *Author's collection*

73

Two-car Hampshire DEMU No. 1121 heads towards Winchester on 1 May 1966 with the 11.09 Alton–Southampton service. It is seen passing the former Butts Junction signal box, which marked the divergence of the Watercress Line from the stub of the former Meon Valley route, which remained open for goods traffic as far as Farringdon. Until closure in 1967, access to the remnant of the former line to Basingstoke, which also diverged here and served Lord Treloar's Hospital, was controlled by a ground frame. *Author's collection*

Merchant Navy Pacific 35008 *Orient Line* forges westwards at Butts Junction with the diverted 10.30 Waterloo–Weymouth service on 15 May 1966. Between the diverging rails is a grindstone used by permanent way men for sharpening tools and scythes when keeping lineside vegetation under control. The first vehicle, identified as No S90S, was an eight-compartment third class vehicle to Bulleid design, built at Eastleigh with seats for sixty-four passengers. Already the difference in levels between the two lines is visible. *Author's collection*

Standard Class 5 No. 73170 brings its lengthy train into the suburbs of Alton on 15 May 1966 with the diverted 14.25 Bournemouth–Waterloo service. *Author's collection*

No. 73113 *Lyonesse* gets to grips with the climb away from Alton with the 11.30 Waterloo–Weymouth service, diverted from its usual route on 5. June 1966. The double track here was operated as two single lines from Alton, following closure of Butts Junction signal box in 1935. Notice also the steel sleepers, a wartime economy measure, on this section of the Meon Valley route and which remained in situ until closure. *Author's collection*

Unusual motive power indeed to grace the Alresford route was Warship D800 *Sir Brian Robertson* seen here passing the well-tended back gardens of houses on the outskirts of Alton with the 07.47 Eastleigh–Waterloo service, on 27 February 1966. *Author's collection*

Unrebuilt Battle of Britain Pacific 34064 *Fighter Command* is wreathed in drifting steam on a wet day piloted out of Alton by D6556 on the 09.33 Waterloo–Bournemouth, 24 April 1966. *Author's collection*

EMU Shunting

We have all heard about it, but in some ways it is a little bit like the 'Indian rope trick', where everyone knows someone else who has seen it – by which I mean using an EMU set for shunting. These two views (above and overleaf) were located at a transport fair some time ago in the 50p box – no annotations or credits on the rear. Clearly taken on a wet day at Wimbledon, unit No 4543 is being used as the depot shunter to move what appear to be empty open wagons and possible stores vans. This immediately raises the question as to the whereabouts of the usual depot shunter DS74 – maintenance, perhaps? Fortunately, even before publication in 'SW' Greg Beecroft has come up with the answer.

'This photograph was published in the June 2007 issue of Live Rail (the magazine of the Southern Electric Group) and there were quite extensive follow-up notes in the April 2008 issue.

'Most importantly, it was established that the photographer was Fred Ivey. In short, No 4543 was one of a number of towing or shunting units used at Strawberry Hill and Durnsford Road depots. It comprised motor coaches Nos 8715 and 8881, which had been converted by the Southern Railway from AC stock and were in use as a shunting unit from September 1956 until May 1959. Towing units were used mainly for moving withdrawn suburban units after traction and control equipment had been removed, particularly from Durnsford Road to Strawberry Hill. No 4543 was officially 'internal user' for shunting at Durnsford Road, with its carriages renumbered 081046 and 081047, but it did in fact work outside the depot from time to time.'

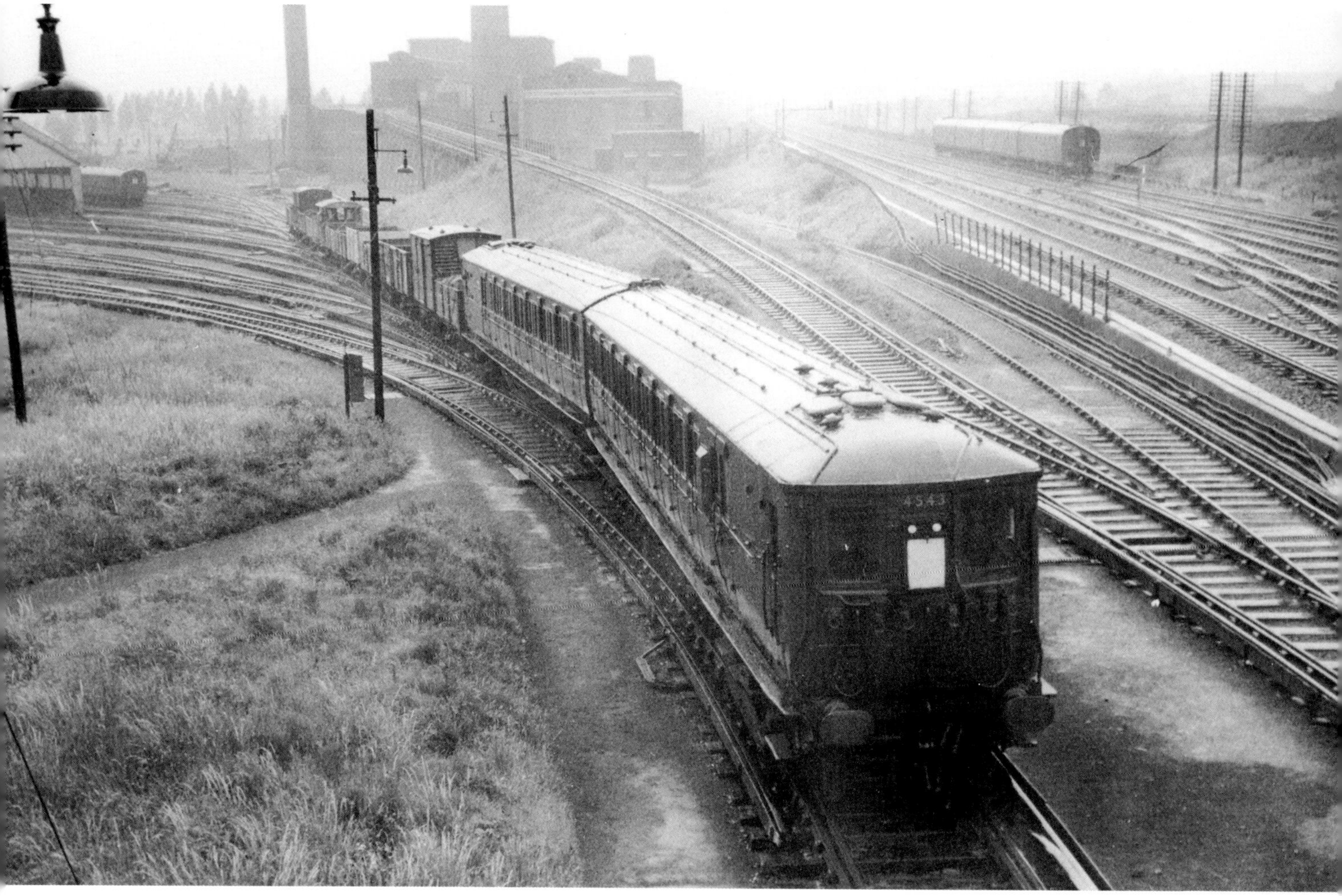

Whistles
Zones of silence

Standard 'Whistle' board at Rotherfield. The locomotive is C Class 0-6-0 No 31590. JJ Smith/Bluebell Railway Museum

Jeremy Staines

'Noise pollution' may well be a phrase more associated with the modern day and yet eighty years ago it was evidently considered an issue, the Southern Railway taking action to curb complaints of excessive engine whistling under the term 'Zones of Silence'.

A recently discovered file of papers gives some detail of how what was considered a problem was dealt with. Interestingly the papers include the phrase 'Ministry of Transport's Proposals: Reduction of Engine Whistling', which indicates that not only had the government somehow become involved but it should also be taken to indicate it was an issue affecting all the railways. However, before describing specific examples we should perhaps look at why engine crews might whistle anyway.

Broadly speaking, engine whistling could be described in one of several categories:

1 – When out on the line to advise of the approach of a train, i.e., approaching a public crossing – a 'whistle' board was invariably provided as a reminder, although the driver was already expected to know this through his route knowledge.

2 – To warn men working on or near the railway

3 – Entering a station where another train might be stationary and there was the risk staff or passengers (in the case of a board crossing) might be near the track. Most level crossings would also come into this category.

4 – When shunting to communicate with staff.

5 – To converse with a signalman, i.e. three short blasts is the accepted means of communication between driver and signalman to indicate the train is clear of a set of points movement, which is otherwise out of sight of the signalman. In this example the provision of a track circuit would obviate this need to whistle but it may simply not be cost-effective to invest in this facility.

6 – As a means of communication between the driver and train guard or the driver and that of an assisting engine. The GWR had a special 'brake' whistle for the driver to communicate with the guard, or in an emergency to advise others the braking capability of the train may be compromised.

7 – As a means of emergency communication, a series of 'pops' on the whistle might be used to indicate to a signalman or station staff that there was a message to impart, 'train running away', or perhaps 'assistance required', by throwing a note attached to a lump of coal as the train passed the signal box or station.

8 – When specified by local instruction. At some locations it was a requirement that a driver whistled when entering or leaving a tunnel.

9 – As a personal means of acknowledgement to other staff or even by means of a private 'code' to communicate with family. This might be used by a driver if he perhaps had a relation working nearby or he lived within 'whistling' distance of the line.

The unmistakable vista of the curving platforms at Southampton Terminus, albeit during BR years and some time after the complaints referred to in the text. The South Western Hotel is the large building above the right-hand canopy; the proximity of which to the station and docks (which lie immediately beyond the station) is immediately apparent. *SWC Eyers collection* (Further views of the Terminus Hotel appear in Part 2 of Alan Postlethwaite's article 'A Review of Southampton's Railways' that appeared in *SW31*.)

All this noise though, especially in categories 4 and 5, could well lead to complaints, as indeed was the case from 1920 onwards at Southampton:

'Southampton Terminus. Numerous complaints have been made by the residents of the South Western Hotel, through the Manager, of the disturbance caused by the sounding of engine whistles at night.

'The regulations respecting the working of traffic over the Harbour Board Tramways require that "the whistle or bell shall be sounded by the driver of the engine from time to time when it is necessary as a warning," and also that the enginemen must sound the engine whistle on approaching or whilst passing the Docks gateway and Post Office building alongside the train line. In order, however, to reduce the amount of whistling, the Western Division Locomotive Running Superintendent in September 1933 issued the following instruction to enginemen: "The whistle is not to be sounded except for the express purpose of warning anyone who would be likely to get foul of the line."

'In August 1934 attention was called by the Parsons Oil Engine Company to the noise resulting from engine whistles in the vicinity of their works at the Town Quay, Southampton. Enquiry was made and it was found that there was no unnecessary use of whistles by drivers having regard to the necessity to warn people and vehicles off the track.'

Neither was Southampton unique as the examples from various years show:

South Croydon – June 1934. 'Complaint was made respecting engines of down trains approaching South Croydon. It transpired that the whistling in connection with distant signals was excessive and a suitable notice was posted at the Locomotive Running Sheds.' The interpretation here is likely to have been that a driver, approaching the location and being faced with the distant signal at 'on', would sound the whistle in the hope of attracting the attention of the signalman to clear the arm. No doubt the signalman would have done so if possible but it only needed one occasion for the whistle to coincide with the signalman being able to pull-off for the message to be passed around other crews. Of course, there was always the case the aforementioned signalman might have been distracted and perhaps needed a reminder! Whilst this specific incident refers to South Croydon, the same scenario would have applied at almost every location, although in a rural situation the noise factor would have been less of a problem. Reading through the 'twenty-five years ago' pages in a local newspaper recently, there was mention of a complaint relating to the sounding of engine whistles on a heritage railway.

August 1925 – 'The Chief Operating Superintendent drew the Electrical Engineer's attention to the fact that many motormen sounded their whistles before starting from every station and Mr Herbert Jones took steps to stop it.' The early LSWR and SR EMU sets had an air-operated whistle rather than a horn.

Devonport – February 1928. 'Residents of Devonport complained respecting whistling in the vicinity of Devonport Junction. On enquiry it transpired that, in the case of down trains, this took place only when the distant signal was in the "on" position while regarding "up" trains, the whistle was necessary for the safety of staff engaged in shunting operations; the cost of installing a warning bell to avoid this was not considered justified.' In the same locality, Plymouth Friary was also an area of complaint caused by engine whistling when shunting. Here an instruction issued on 24 January 1935 reduced the number of whistle codes applicable and with three exceptions prohibited any whistling between 10.30pm and 4.30am.

Lymington branch – July 1929. 'Complaint was made regarding engines of Lymington branch trains whistling when approaching Pensford Road bridge in accordance with an instruction which appeared in the LSWR Appendix, May 1894. As opinion was that this was in connection with horse traffic and the Company was not under any legal obligation to give warning, the instruction referred to was cancelled.'

Holborn Low Level, 1929 onwards. 'Complaints were made from time to time by tenants and others in the London Central Meat Market respecting the noise caused through the exchange of whistles between trains and bank engines of foreign companies' goods trains about to proceed to Ludgate Hill. A scheme was prepared for the installation of light indicators to enable the necessary exchange of signals between the drivers to be made in lieu of whistling but in view of the heavy expenditure involved the matter is in abeyance.'

Preston Park – August 1930. 'A complaint was received regarding the whistling of engines in the neighbourhood of Preston Park. The matter was taken up with the Locomotive Running Superintendent who, after investigation, stated there was not much cause for complaint but that a suitable notice had been issued to enginemen.'

Cannon Street – March 1931. 'Complaint by a passenger of whistling by engines working trains from Cannon Street. As a result of enquiry it was found that no unnecessary whistling took place.'

Woking, July 1931. 'Complaint was made respecting the whistling in the vicinity of the Junction box up main home signals. The whistling was due to the observance of Rule 55 by the drivers of trains stopping at the signals, and in order to obviate this special train waiting apparatus was provided in August 1931 and an instruction issued exempting drivers from sounding the engine whistle in accordance with the rule.'

Herne Hill, May 1933. 'Complaint was received from residents in the vicinity of Herne Hill station of the disturbance caused by shunting operations and the whistling of engines. Instructions were issued to the staff concerned to carry out the work as quickly as possible.'

Reigate, August 1933. 'A complaint was received of the whistling of engines in the vicinity of Reigate. The matter was taken up with the Locomotive Running Department and instructions were issued to drivers that whistling would be kept to a minimum.'

Exeter Central, August 1934. 'Complaint was received

Exeter Central: the location where Mrs Diggens was the complainant in 1934. W Class 2-6-4T No 31911 is reversing back to St David's, having banked a train up to Central. *SWC Eyers collection*

regarding the whistling of engines in the vicinity of Exeter Central station. Enquiry revealed that this was due to the observance of Rule 55 by the drivers of trains detained at the "A" signal box down outer home signal. The matter is under investigation.' Exeter was the only place where the name of the complainant was given, Mrs Diggens. She is believed to have lived in Hillsborough Avenue, which backed on to the railway between Exeter Central and St James Park Halt and who, it was reported, had written several letters of complaint on the same subject.

Bromley South, August 1934. 'Complaint was made regarding whistling near Bromley South station. The attention of the Locomotive Running Superintendent was called to the matter, who has issued a suitable instruction to enginemen.

'In all cases where complaint is lodged, enquiry is made with the Locomotive Running Department and, whenever necessary, suitable instructions are issued with a view to the use of engine whistles being reduced to a minimum.

'The general instructions respecting engine whistles are contained on pages 153–4 in the Central-Eastern Appendix and pages 144–6 of the Western Appendix, from which it will be seen that, as a general principal, engine whistles are sounded only when signals are in the "on" position, but in certain cases, i.e., when sounded as a warning to staff or approaching level crossing, the whistles are always to be given. In the case of many level crossings, especially on light railways where gates are not provided, it is a statutory requirement that the engine whistle of all trains should be sounded for the periods indicated in the Appendix.

'It may be noted, however, that instructions are already extant that the whistle code at Bournemouth Central loco is not to be used between 10.00pm and 6.00am.

'At Waterloo, Victoria (Central and Eastern sections), Brighton, London Bridge and Portsmouth Harbour exemption is given from the exchange of whistles required by Rule 133(c)

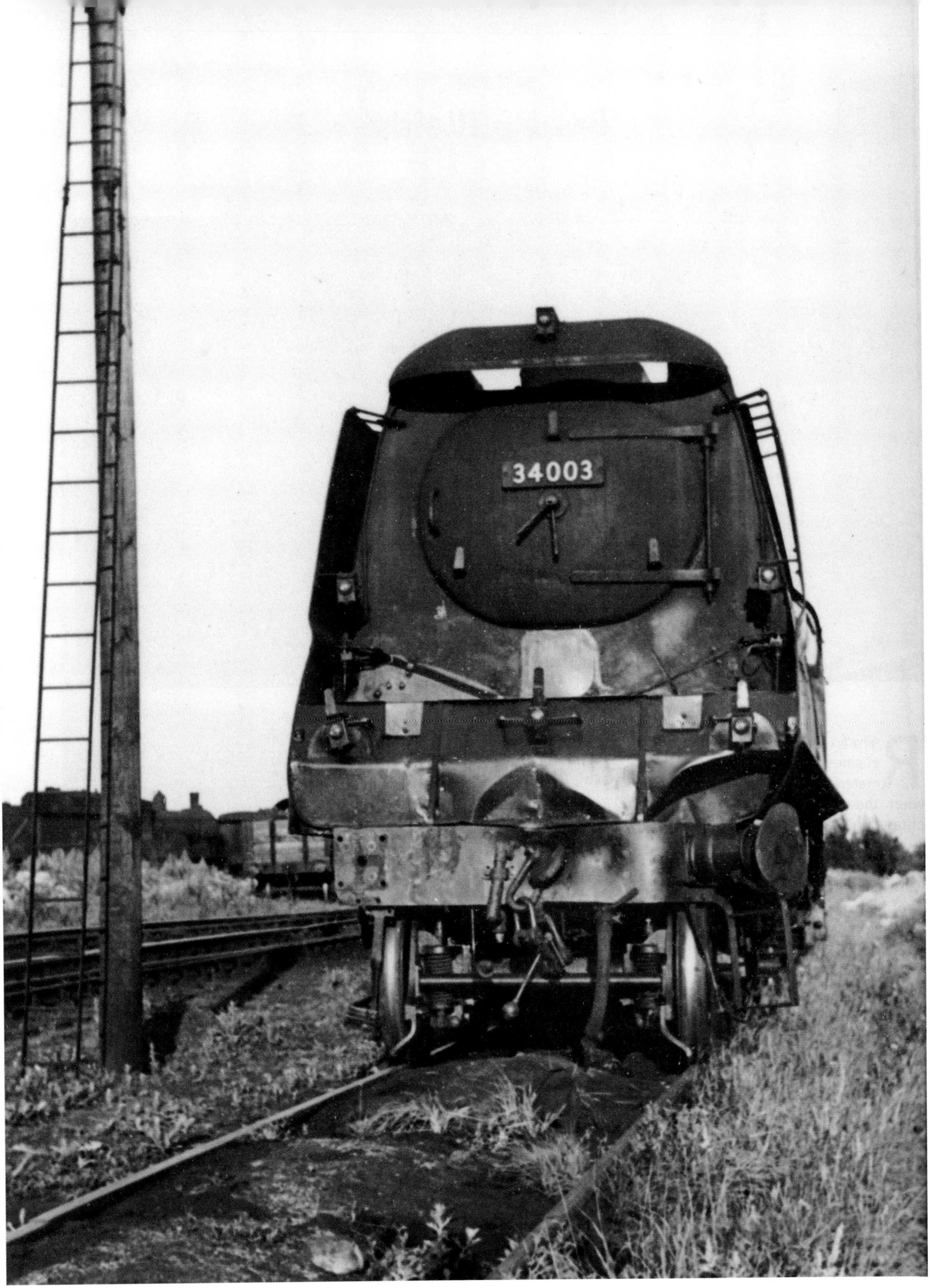
34003

Colour Interlude
Just one station ...

Trawling through the Roger Holmes collection, we were delighted to find a selection of detailed views of Chandlers Ford (modellers will recall the highly talented Martyn Welch used the buildings as the basis for his inspirational 'Hursley' layout). So with that in mind, perhaps the next selection may provide some inspiration for a new generation...

As a modelling prototype, it could be ideal, a country location but one on which locomotives of all sizes might be seen. Apart from the yellow BR litter bin and a few posters, the whole thing is timeless – pure Southern Railway – and of course it is the original Chandlers Ford, not the replacement that was erected on what is now just a single (but very useful) line. Speaking to Martyn Welch reference these same images, he recounted how he had once been approached at an exhibition and regaled with the story of how this particular individual had been to Hursley village and reported he had found what he said was the derelict station site. (Hursley never did have a railway... .)

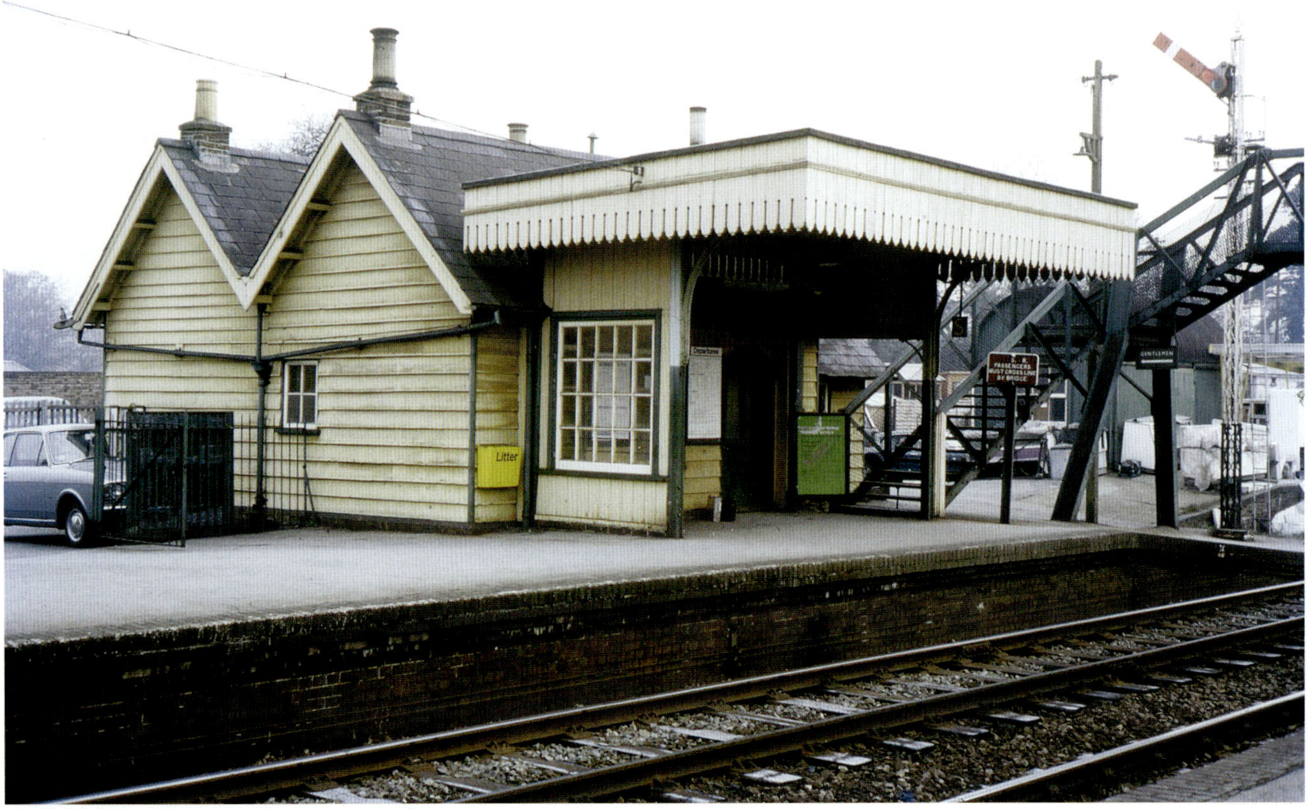
Litter
GENTLEMEN

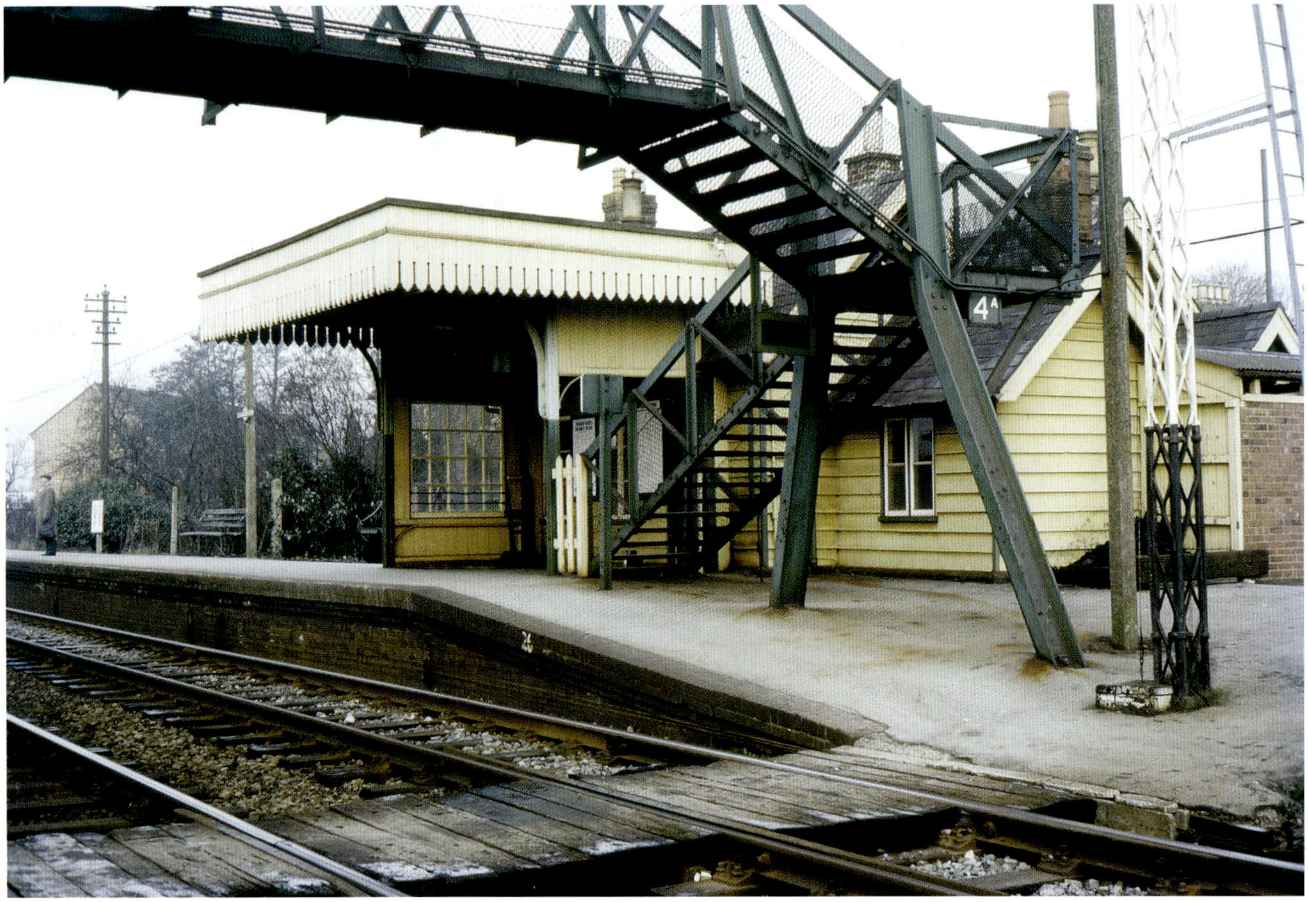
4A

Colour interlude

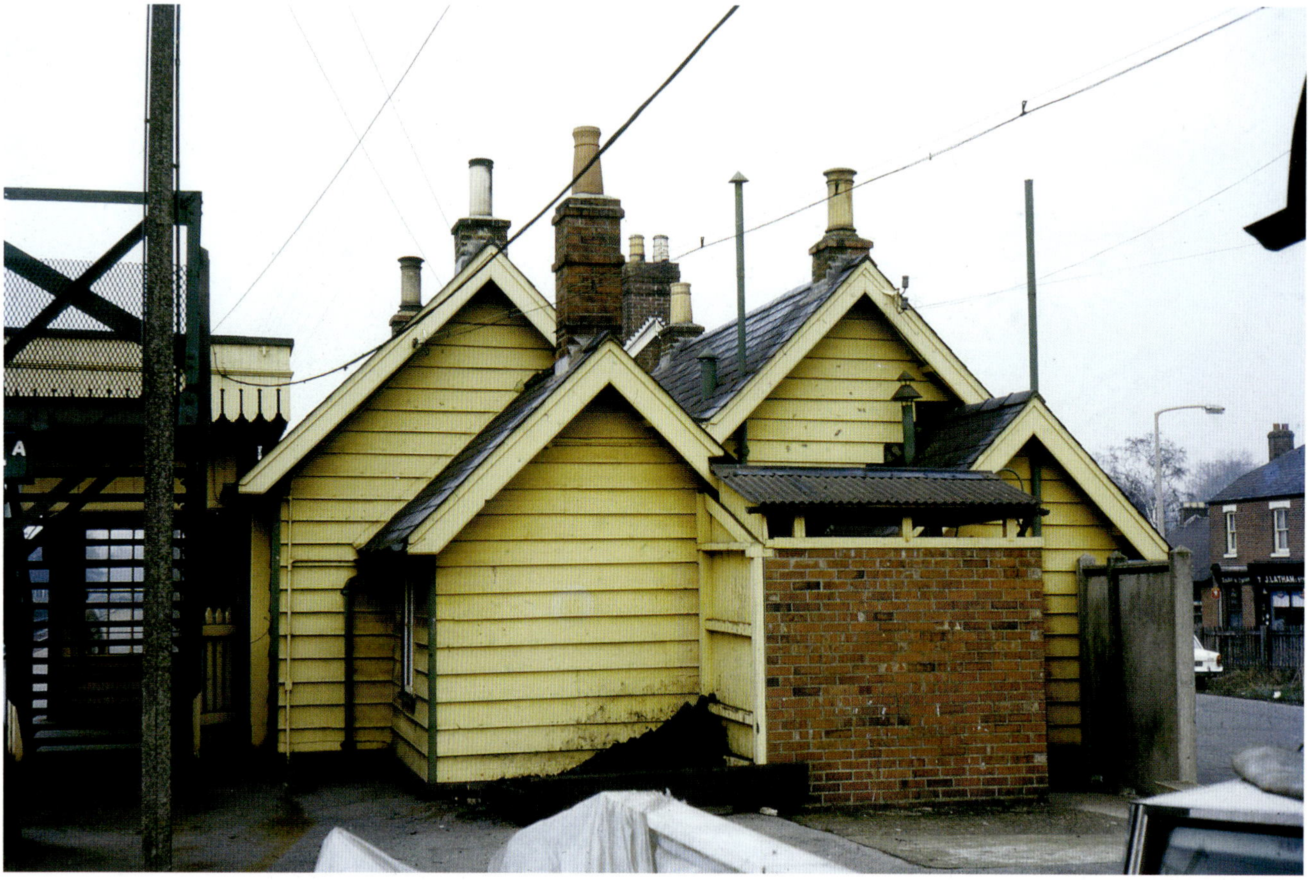

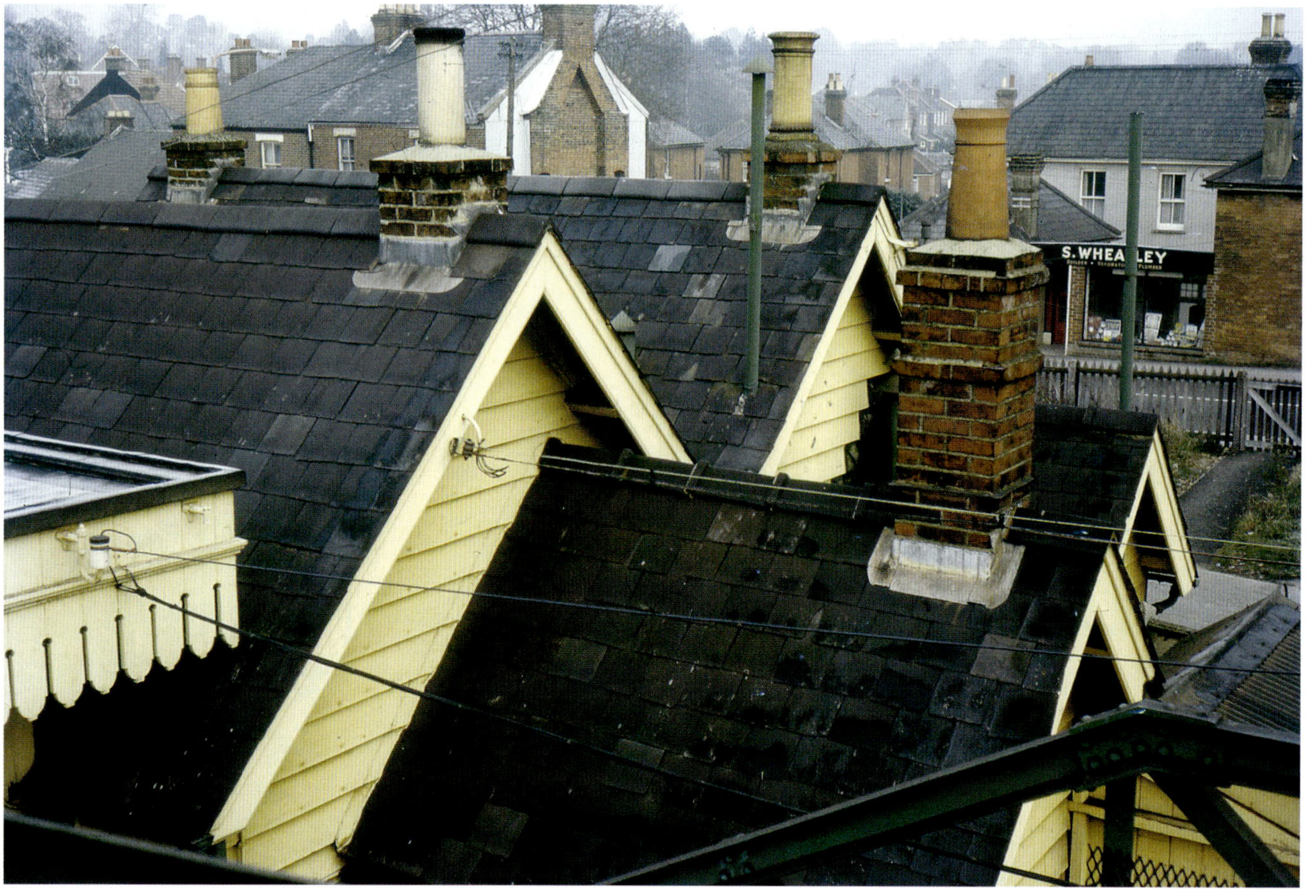

Colour interlude

The Purbeck Clay Express!

Jeff Grayer

A Manning Wardle 0-4-ST (Works No 1552) of 1902 vintage was purchased by the Fayles Tramway in 1909 from the Northern Outfall Sewerage line of London County Council at Barking and subsequently converted from 2ft 6in to 3ft 9in gauge.

The engine was bought specifically for the long haul to Goathorn, as it was too high to pass under the road bridge between Norden depot and the exchange siding, although the track here was later lowered under the bridge to enable it to do so. The locomotive retained the name *Thames* from its previous life on cast plates attached to the saddle tanks, with No 48 on the cabside. It was famously used to run the line's passenger service, using a converted clay wagon with a corrugated iron roof known locally as 'The Hen House'.

Newton School, which was used as a chapel on Sundays before a purpose-built chapel was built and consecrated in February 1920, had been closed for some time when the Hen House conveyed schoolchildren daily from Newton to Corfe Castle school for a return fare of 7s 6d per week from June 1934. This was to encourage attendance at school for the children, who should have gone to Studland school, some considerable walk away, and had not attended school for a year. The school children alighted from the train at Arfleet and walked into Corfe to the junior and senior schools in East Street. An extra shed was built opposite the locomotive shed where the Newton link line met the Nordem workings, to accommodate the 'coach'. When the train ceased running in January 1937, the children returned to Studland school but by taxi instead of shanks's pony. The locomotive was scrapped in 1948. The ensemble plus schoolchildren is shown here. *Jeffery Grayer collection*

The Southern Way

The regular volume for the Southern devotee

BACK ISSUES

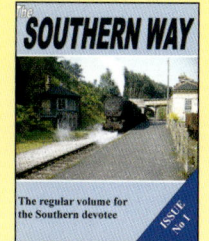

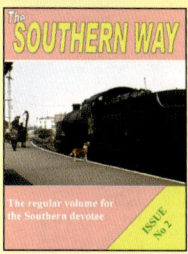

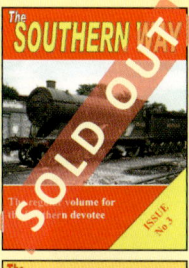

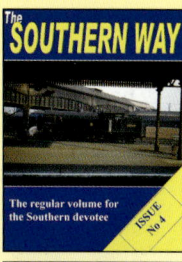

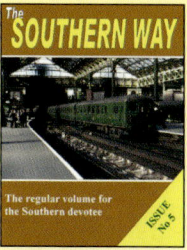

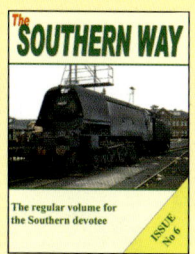

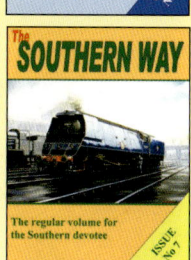

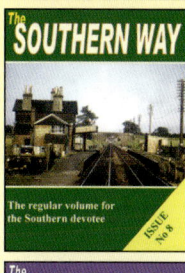

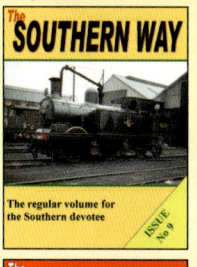

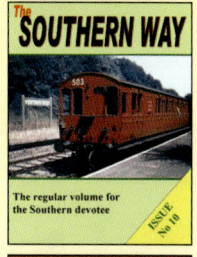

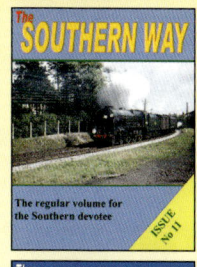

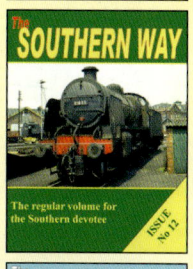

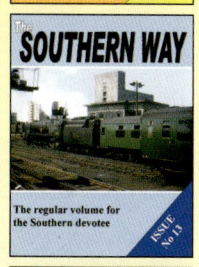

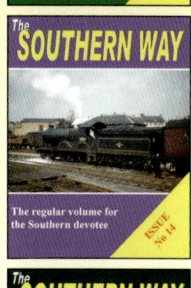

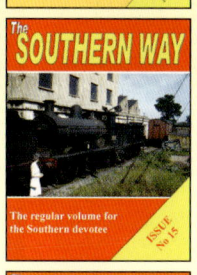

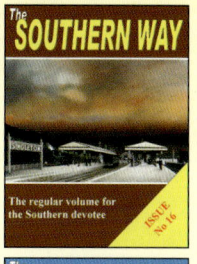

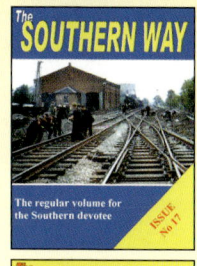

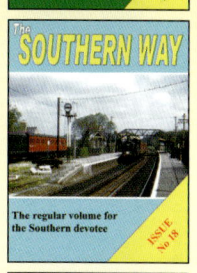

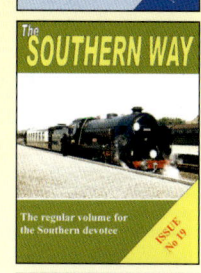

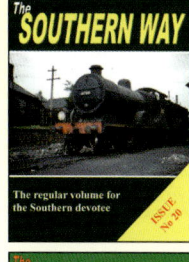

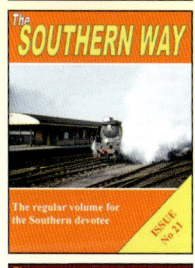

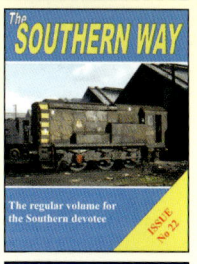

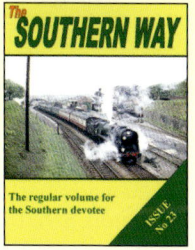

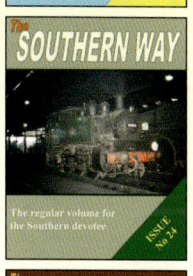

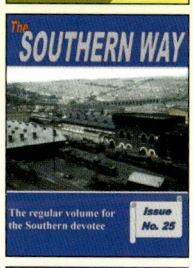

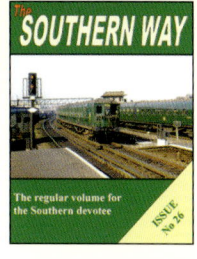

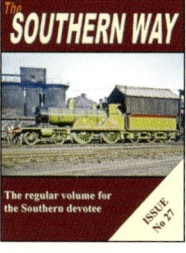

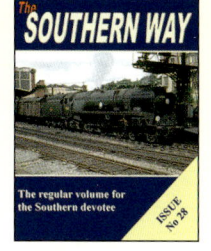

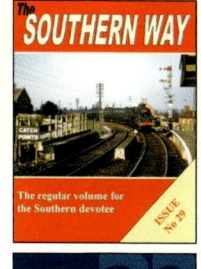

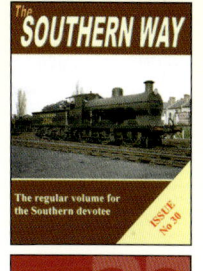

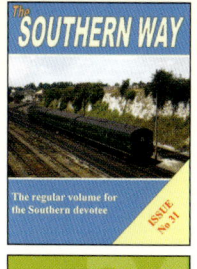

The Southern Way is available from all good book sellers, or in case of difficulty, direct from the publisher. (Post free UK) Each regular issue contains at least 96 pages including colour content.

£11.95 each
£12.95 from Issue 7
£14.50 from Issue 21

Subscription for four-issues available (Post free in the UK)

www.crecy.co.uk

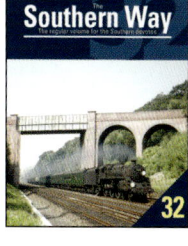

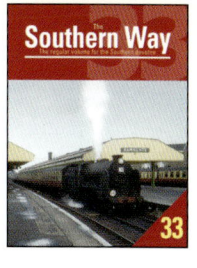

95

The Southern Way
The regular volume for the Southern devotee

SPECIAL ISSUES

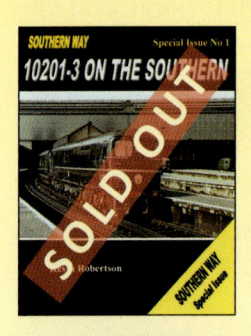

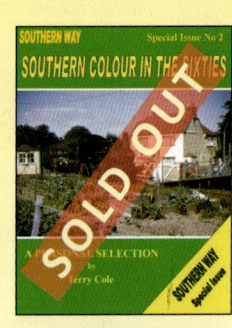

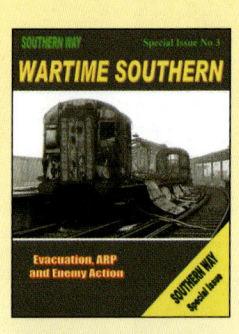

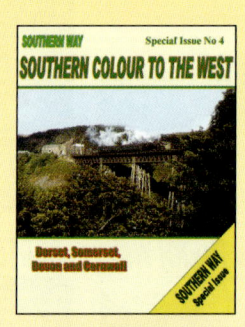

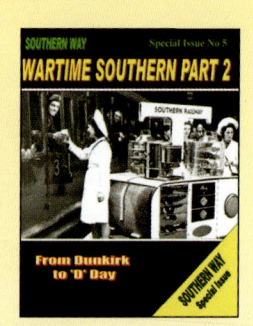

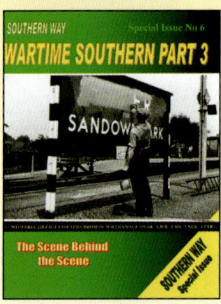

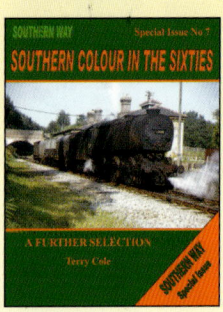

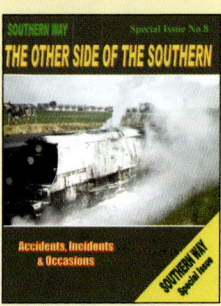

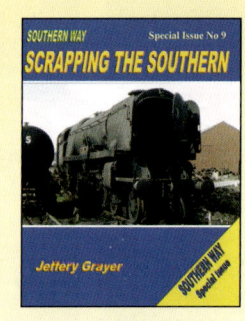

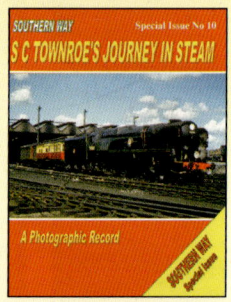

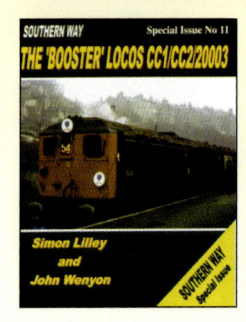

SOUTHERN WAY 'Special Issues'
Nos 3 to 5 £14.95. Nos 6 to 12 £16.50

Editorial matters only to: editorial@thesouthernway.co.uk
01489 877880 or by post to:

The Southern Way (Kevin Robertson)
PO Box 279, Corhampton, SOUTHAMPTON SO32 3ZX

Orders, subscriptions and sales enquiries to:

Crécy Publishing, 1a Ringway Trading Est, Shadowmoss Rd, Manchester, M22 5LH

0161 499 0024

www.crecy.co.uk

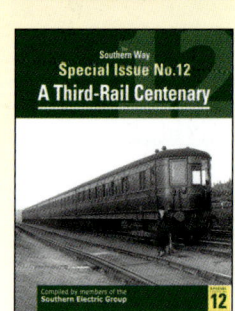